Praise for *Defending W*

'It says something about the alarming
live that a book like this has to be written. Who would have thought that, 40 years after the start of second-wave feminism, we would have to go back to first principles by defending all over again the women-only spaces that were created as a prerequisite to achieving women's autonomy, equality and freedom – a struggle that remains not only unfinished business but is now under huge multi-directional threat? Karen Ingala Smith makes a clear and powerful case for the right of women to have a room of our own, not as part of some crude competition for the status of ultimate victimhood or to prioritise the human rights of women over others, but as a key site of feminist resistance against patriarchal violence and sex-based oppression. Let's read, discuss and even agree to disagree, but let's do it with honesty, decency and compassion, and without descending into the blind alley of regressive identity politics.'

Pragna Patel, founder and ex-director
of Southall Black Sisters

'A lucid and insightful defence of women's sex-based rights and the need for single-sex services for women who have been subjected to male violence and abuse written by someone who has worked in the sector for three decades.'

Joanna Cherry KC MP

'Karen Ingala Smith is a giant in women's safety: few have done more to fight for women's lives and voices to count. She is unapologetically women-focused.'

Jess Phillips MP

'Karen is a true feminist, gutsy and determined and forcing us to confront the terrible extent of violence against women and girls carried out every single day in the UK. Her book is accessible, sometimes brutal, but delivered in her own style as a very funny and incredibly likeable woman. Direct, punchy and readable, this book presents things all women should know.'

Rosie Duffield MP

'This authoritative book marshals all the evidence for providing single-sex spaces for women traumatised by male violence – and for excluding transwomen, that is males who identify as women, from such spaces. Ingala Smith is one of Britain's foremost campaigners against male violence, and as chief executive of one of the few organisations supporting women victims of men's violence to stand up publicly for female-only spaces, she has played a key role in the recent resurgence of feminist activism in opposition to trans ideology. Her deep knowledge and crisp, clean prose make this both an essential and enjoyable read.'

Helen Joyce, author of *Trans: When Ideology Meets Reality*

'*Defending Women's Spaces* is an important, factual, and therefore appropriately chilling account of how gender identity politics has destroyed women's safe spaces and challenged our feminist understanding of women's sex-based rights. Essential reading.'

Phyllis Chesler, author of *Women and Madness*
and *A Politically Incorrect Feminist*

'Karen Ingala Smith makes a compelling argument in favour of female-only spaces and services. Her practical insights, derived from three decades of experience working for women, provide an important and welcome intervention into the academic debates around gender. This book will also force policy-makers to recognize how sex matters.'

Michael Biggs, Associate Professor of Sociology and
Fellow of St Cross College, University of Oxford

Defending Women's Spaces

Defending Women's Spaces

KAREN INGALA SMITH

polity

First published in 2023 by Polity Press

Polity Press
65 Bridge Street
Cambridge CB2 1UR, UK

Polity Press
111 River Street
Hoboken, NJ 07030, USA

ISBN-13: 978-1-5095-5443-0
ISBN-13: 978-1-5095-5444-7 (pb)

A catalogue record for this book is available from the British Library.

Library of Congress Control Number: 2022940799

Typeset in 11 on 14 pt Warnock Pro
by Cheshire Typesetting Ltd, Cuddington, Cheshire
Printed and bound in Great Britain by TJ Books Limited, Padstow, Cornwall

The publisher has used its best endeavours to ensure that the URLs for external websites referred to in this book are correct and active at the time of going to press. However, the publisher has no responsibility for the websites and can make no guarantee that a site will remain live or that the content is or will remain appropriate.

Every effort has been made to trace all copyright holders, but if any have been overlooked the publisher will be pleased to include any necessary credits in any subsequent reprint or edition.

For further information on Polity, visit our website:
politybooks.com

For any woman who is a victim/survivor of men's violence and who has ever wanted a space away from men

For any woman who has said no to men in her space or space for her sisters

For any woman who has been told that in wanting to be in a space without men, she is the one with the problem

Contents

Acknowledgements

I'd like to sincerely thank the following women for sharing their thoughts and stories, and using their expertise to help me bridge some of the gaps in my knowledge or access their transcripts (any remaining errors are mine, however): Keira Bell, Nicola Benge, Leonora Christina, Edith Eligator, For Women Scotland, Cátia Freitas, Dawn Fyfe, Judith Green, Scarlet Harris, Jean Hatchet, Rachel Hewitt, Emma Hilton, Onjali Raúf, Hannana Siddiqui, Sarah Summers, Still Tish, Kruti Walsh, Verdi Wilson, Bec Wonders; also to the women I spoke with who asked to maintain anonymity: I want to thank you all for your insight, contributions and support, and acknowledge its worth; nia's senior management team and trustees: Sophia Antoniazzi, Dana Baldwin, Marcia Buxton, Louise Campbell, Nadine Evans, Rachel Evans, Heather Harvey, Caroline Murphy, Felicity Slater, Amy Terry, Ruth Tweedale and Jodie Woodward for committing to prioritising women and taking on whatever came our way and for supporting me in the writing of this book; for holding the line for so long: Vancouver Rape Relief and Women's Shelter; for sisterhood, support, solidarity and all you do for women: WPUK and the women who have spoken for and supported us, Lisa-Marie

Taylor, Julie Bindel; for approaching me about the possibility of writing this book and for your skilful editing which hugely improved my initial manuscript, Elise Heslinga; for encouraging me to agree to write this book when the timing was dreadful: Clarrie O'Callaghan and Ruth Tweedale (I've cursed you both a few times); for representing and supporting me, Caroline Hardman; for commenting on early drafts and helping me improve the manuscript (and the rest): Shonagh Dillon, Jayne Egerton, Samm Goodall (and the last two for being my adopted Amiga Sisters); for four decades of friendship and all that's come with it: Kirsten Durrans; for everything they've done to make me who I am, my parents Susan French and Bruno Ingala. And last, but definitely not least, for being the reason that I feel happy whenever I put my key in the front door or hear his: André Smith.

1

What is the Problem?

In January 2016, the UK government's Women and Equalities Committee (WESC) published the Transgender Equality Report. The report claimed that each of us is assigned sex at birth and quotes a newspaper article which claims that it is a 'sobering and distressing fact that in UK surveys of trans people about half of young people and a third of adults report that they have attempted suicide'. Speaking of the single-sex exceptions permitted in the Equality Act 2010, the report states that the Act permits service providers not to allow a trans person to access separate-sex or single-sex services – on a case-by-case basis. Quotes in this section included comments from an anonymous individual who likened the permitted exclusion of transgender people to apartheid, from the Scottish Transgender Alliance recommending the removal of the single-sex exceptions from domestic violence and abuse refuges and rape crisis services, and from Galop, an LGBT anti-abuse charity, which claimed that transgender people are currently at serious risk of harm by being excluded from such services. One respondent, Mridul Wadhwa, had written with regard to employment in 'the gender-based violence sector', 'I am disappointed to think that someone has the right to refuse work to me and others like me in my sector just because they think that I might not be a woman.'[1] This book makes the case for why I disagree and is a defence of women-only spaces.

I will begin by asserting that human beings are not assigned a sex at birth, but that our biological sex is observed and recorded. Our biological sex is in reality determined by our chromosomes at fertilisation, and sex differentiation in an embryo begins after 6–7 weeks of gestation.[2] In chapter 7, I will take a closer look at the statistics on suicide and transgender youth and show that the claim above has no place being reported as fact in a report from a government inquiry. Throughout the book I will aim to explain why allowing biological males with transgender identities to access women's spaces poses a serious potential risk to women's safety, well-being and recovery.

Seventy-four per cent of all victims of recorded domestic abuse-related offences against adults aged between 16 and 74 years in England and Wales were female.[3] Ninety-two per cent of defendants in domestic abuse-related prosecutions in England and Wales were males.[4] Ninety-eight per cent of perpetrators of rapes and assaults by penetration in England and Wales were male.[5] Ninety-five per cent of those exploited in prostitution are female.[6] Girls are at least three times more likely than boys to report experiences of child sexual abuse.[7]

Globally, 27 per cent (more than a quarter) of women aged under fifty are estimated to have been subjected to physical or sexual, or both, intimate partner violence in their lifetime, 13 per cent in the year prior to being surveyed. Twenty-four per cent of girls and young women aged 15–19 years old and 26 per cent of women aged 19–24 had experienced this violence and abuse at least once by the time they were 15 years old.[8]

Men's violence against women and girls is both a manifestation of sex inequality and a way in which sex inequality is maintained. Men's violence against women is more than a number of individual acts perpetrated by individual men, though of course every man should be held to account for what he does. It is a social and political issue and it is for this reason that we need to address the circumstances that are conducive to it.[9] Whether or not individual men pose harm, it benefits women if all males are excluded from some spaces. Equally when we think about men who are abusive in relationships, we shouldn't characterise their behaviour as a series of isolated incidents. Domestic abuse is a way that women are diminished and controlled; violence can be part of that control. Perpetrators routinely fail to recognise this. If they admit to violence, they are more likely to excuse it as an out-of-character outburst, something that is rare, rather than something that fits within the pattern of how they operate in a relationship, and something that reflects broader patterns of men's violence against women. Power and control are the endgames. Sociologist Sylvia Walby talked about private and public patriarchy: private patriarchy being what happens in many heterosexual homes, public patriarchy being what happens in the world outside.[10] The personal is political. Women learn how to modify their behaviour, how to avoid upsetting their partner, and to put his needs first. Outside the home, women make innumerable small or large modifications to what we do to try to keep ourselves safe. All men benefit from the sex inequality maintained by men's violence against women and girls.

Feminism is not a monolith. There is no prescribed set of rules and no single way of doing feminism. However, this book reflects the ways I've come to approach feminism. Debate exists within feminism about whether we should be revolutionaries or reformists. Revolutionaries recognise that patriarchal society is the core or root of the problem and that equality in this society is an impossible dream. A reformist position would be to chip away at what is wrong with our society, try to squeeze a few women (usually those privileged in some way) into roles usually occupied by men and gradually create one that is not so hostile to women. In reality, most feminists are a combination of both and most radical feminists also recognise the value of reform. The feminists who created refuges[11] and rape support services recognised this. Specialist services for women who had been subjected to men's violence were needed – and are still needed – because of what men do to women, girls and children. It never meant that they accepted that men's violence against women and girls was inevitable and could not be ended.

It is incorrect to claim that there is no clash between a feminism which targets sex-based oppression and gender identity ideology,[12] or that there is no clash between women's sex-based rights and protections and some of the prospective extensions of trans rights. This book is primarily about why we need women-only, that is single-sex, spaces, particularly specialist services led by women, which are delivered by women, to women who are victim-survivors of men's violence. I look at how they were developed through an incredible wave of feminist activism and how the state then assumed ownership of what women created. I will look at the threat posed to single-sex services by transgender rights activism and ask what has happened to the feminist spirit in the movement responding to men's violence against women? How has this movement reached the point where many refuse – whether through capitulation or conviction – to say that women are adult human females? That women's oppression is based on our sex and that some of the needs of women are best met in single-sex services.

The importance of women-only space goes beyond the needs of women who have been subjected to men's violence. Conflicts about males who self-identify as women mainly fall into two categories: practical considerations about mixed sex spaces and more abstract concerns over social justice and fairness. However, this book deals mainly with the first. Physical spaces and services include hospital wards, prisons, support or counselling groups, changing rooms, toilets, women-only leisure services such as gym classes or swimming pools, conferences and meetings, schools and training; or the provision of personal or medical care, sports categories, prizes, shortlists or awards for women; or particular jobs. In the UK, some of these are covered by the Equality Act 2010, and the single-sex exceptions justify excluding males if doing so is a proportionate means of achieving a legitimate aim and if at least one of six qualifying criteria are met:

1. only people of that sex require it;
2. there is joint provision for both sexes but that is not sufficient on its own;
3. if the service were provided for men and women jointly, it would not be as effective and it is not reasonably practicable to provide separate services for each sex;
4. they are provided in a hospital or other place where users need special attention;
5. they may be used by more than one person and a woman might object to the presence of a man (or vice versa); or
6. they may involve physical contact between a user and someone else and that other person may reasonably object if the user is of the opposite sex.

The explanatory notes[13] go on to give examples where this is lawful, such as in cervical cancer screening services, domestic violence support service, hospital wards, changing rooms in department stores. These are examples, rather than being a list of the only possible exceptions. The single-sex exceptions mean that the prohibition of gender reassignment discrimination does not apply in these circumstances; instead, sex is given precedence over gender reassignment. In 2022, the UK's Equality and Human Rights Commission issued new guidance on interpretation of the Equality Act and the single-sex exceptions. The guidance made more explicit the legitimacy of women-only space in qualifying circumstances.[14]

However, using the Act still isn't mandatory, so there are cases where the single-sex exceptions could be applied and haven't been. Some organisations or individuals have decided to include males with transgender identities in their women-only spaces or categories on the understanding that 'transwomen are women', even where the Act would permit their exclusion and where some women would prefer the space to be for females only. Though I focus on the needs of women who have been subjected to sexual and domestic violence and abuse, I will address some of these other areas too.

This book prioritises women, and in so doing is not 'anti-trans'. Certain aspects of what I term 'transgender ideology' or 'transgender identity ideology', however, create an environment that is arguably hostile to specialist single-sex services for women who have been subjected to men's violence and one in which women cannot set our own boundaries – and this is what I object to. Equally, to dismiss the perspective of female victim-survivors as underpinned by 'misandry' or irrational fear is to deny their clarity of vision which has come from hard-won insight, while to class the legitimate protections they ask for as transphobic oppression misrepresents reality.

Part of the problem is that some people use the terms 'sex' and 'gender' as if they were the same. They are not. 'Gender' slipped into usage in some circumstances to avoid saying or writing the word 'sex', and it's just a few steps from this until the word woman becomes a social rather than a biological category. The Gender Recognition Act (GRA) further complicates things because it permits those who obtain a Gender Recognition Certificate (GRC) to change their sex as recorded on official documents such as birth certificates, passports and driving licences. When I talk about women-only spaces, I mean single-sex spaces. From my perspective, a space which includes biological males who identify as women should be recognised as a mixed-sex space. When I say transgender male, I mean someone who is biologically male rather than someone who identifies as male. I don't use terms like 'cis', 'cisgender' and 'cis woman', since, in my view, this prefix suggests that adult human females – in my view, women – are a sub-section of their own category. I will not uphold this perspective, nor use such terms. If we accept the concept of cis women, we're accepting that the class of 'woman' can be mixed-sex.

I choose to talk about 'men's violence' rather than 'male violence', because I do not accept that the biology of males determines their propensity to be violent to women. Maleness is a biological characteristic; manliness, or masculinity, is something else. However, being male in combination with the effects of socialisation – the process in which a male infant becomes an adult man – means that biology does play a significant and undeniable role in the nature of that violence. Another undeniable fact is that males who transition share the biology of those who do not, and it is impossible to meaningfully alter the consequences of that biology.[15]

When I talk about women who have been subjected to men's violence, I use the word 'subjected' deliberately to convey that the violence was done to them by someone. If we say women who have experienced violence, we linguistically make invisible the fact that someone was responsible. But it didn't just happen out of nowhere. I talk about women victim-survivors, as some women see themselves as one or the other, or sometimes as moving from victim to survivor. Some women reject being seen as a victim, while others believe that the word victim should be destigmatised, and that discomfort around identifying someone as a victim is itself a form of judgement. And of course, some women do not survive.

Throughout this book, I am almost always talking about males who believe or say they believe they have transitioned to being a woman, or transwomen. I focus on this group because it is almost always males who are seeking to breach boundaries set up to protect women, so females who transition are not a meaningful object of focus in this context. From my perspective, 'transmen' remain female. I would not seek to exclude them from women-only spaces and recognise that they are harmed by gendered stereotypes, as are all women. Arguments that their presence may be triggering to women, for example because they may have an altered and masculine appearance, can in some cases, be approached in the same way as we would to similar arguments about other women who chose not to adopt stereotypically female traits. However, we must also recognise that some females have altered their appearance to the extent that their appearance to other women is as if they were male. Here, some compromise has to be made and, unfortunately, someone's needs must be prioritised.

The British Triathlon Federation, the national governing body for Triathlon, Aquathlon and Duathlon in Great Britain released a statement in July 2022, saying that they had reviewed their Transgender Policy and would, from 2023, be introducing two categories of competitors: females and 'an Open Category (for all individuals including male, transgender and those non-binary who were male sex at birth)'. They reaffirmed their commitment to sports for all and that transphobic behaviour, harassment, bullying or hate speech would not be tolerated.[16] To me, extending this approach, encouraging males to accept other (males) who do not conform to the stereotypes associated with their sex, is a welcome way forward: recognising the rights of all whilst not denying the realities of biological sex. In some circumstances, particularly those where safety is a concern, another option might be to look at so-called 'third spaces'. For example, Fionne Orlander and Miranda Yardley, both transwomen, say

> In recognition that women should have access to single sex spaces, and in recognition of our own concern and fear of using single sex spaces designated for males, we call on all political parties to recognise the need for the provision of publicly funded third spaces for transgender individuals of either sex, to allow us to participate fully in public life without imposing ourselves on those single sex places presently enjoyed by women.[17]

I would take this a step further: if we need third spaces for people with transgender identities, this should not mean that females who have undergone gender reassignment forego their right to single-sex spaces, particularly if they come to regret the steps they have taken. Perhaps, therefore, sometimes, we need third and fourth spaces.

The advantages of third (or fourth) spaces would be that all are kept safe. It would not matter whether the transgender identity was a result of dysphoria or ill-intent. The potential risks to women that have been increased by permitting males with transgender identities into public spaces such as toilets, would be removed, if, of course, the third space was used in line with the intended purpose. There may be resistance from some trans rights activists as the space would not function to affirm or validate desires. Third/fourth spaces should not prevent us from addressing other needs that have been ignored because of sex-role stereotyping, such as the assumption that males would not have child-care responsibilities, and third spaces would also address inconveniences associated with that. There may also be resistance from those who would see this as reinforcing the legitimacy of gender identity. And, of course there would be a cost, but that should not be used as a reason to fail to protect people's dignity and safety. We are accustomed to building hygiene facilities into public spaces and for the requirements of those spaces to change over time, and the vast resources of activist lobby groups could be effectively mobilised towards this end.

It is argued that the words 'women' and 'man' are defined socially. The GRA makes provision for some people to be defined socially and legally as that which they are not biologically, but most people relate this social category to the biological equivalents: female and male. My take on Simone de Beauvoir's famous proclamation that 'One is not born, but rather becomes, a woman' is not that we should be tempted to divorce womanhood from biology but to draw attention to the multitude of ways in which our physical, female bodies take on meaning as they move through the social world. Or, as Germaine Greer said, 'Just because you lop off your dick and then wear a dress doesn't make you a fucking woman. I've asked my doctor to give me long ears and liver spots and I'm going to wear a brown coat but that won't turn me into a fucking cocker spaniel.'[18]

The idea of a female brain has been used to justify sexism and misogyny for centuries. In 1912, Lord Curzon, former MP for the Conservative Party, who opposed women's right to vote said, 'Women have not, as a sex or a class, the calmness of temperament or the balance of mind required to make political judgements.'[19] Despite feminists' efforts towards making this line of argument obsolete, some trans rights activists continue to push the idea that some essence of gender is innate.

A claim made by some trans rights activists is that some people are born into the wrong body,[20] though this appears to be asserted less frequently than it was in the past; others that the concept of binary sex is a tool of white colonialist supremacy,[21] or that the category of woman is not fixed and should be 'expanded to include (those) new possibilities'.[22] All of this has been used as reasons for arguing that 'transwomen are women' and therefore should, 'as women', be included in women-only spaces. Kathleen Stock's *Material Girls* persuasively counters Judith Butler's assertion that males should be included in the category of woman.[23] Meanwhile, Gina Rippon[24] and Cordelia Fine[25] convincingly debunk the notion of the gendered brain, and illustrate that it is cultural beliefs about sex – in other words, gender – that are socially constructed, rather than sex itself. Other research has shown that when children are introduced to fictional characters who challenge stereotypes, their own endorsement of them declines.[26]

Rippon describes the brain as a rule scavenger which picks up its rules from the outside world. The rules will change how the brain works and how someone behaves. The upshot of gendered rules? 'The "gender gap" becomes a self-fulfilling prophecy.' She said,

> We need to persistently challenge gender stereotypes. We can see how they are shaping the lives of young children, how they are serving as gatekeepers to the higher echelons of power, politics, business, science as well as possibly contributing to mental health conditions such as depression or eating disorders.[27]

For Cordelia Fine,

> The circuits of the brain are quite literally a product of your physical, social, and cultural environment, as well as your behaviour and your thoughts . . . Neuroscience is used by some in a way that it has often been used in the past: to reinforce, with all the authority of science, old fashioned stereotypes and roles . . . The gender equality you see is in your mind. So are the cultural beliefs about gender that are so familiar to us all.[28]

Of course, most of us, as younger and older adults have opportunities to challenge and unlearn the stereotypes that we learned as children, perhaps in a more conscious way than in early childhood when lessons are unconsciously absorbed. But 'appropriate' (that is, stereotypical) behaviours are learned early and they are learned deeply. By the time we are teenagers or adults, let alone 40-year-old males, most of us have absorbed the gendered behaviour stereotypes associated with either sex, but, crucially, usually see these as our innate personality characteristics. This is not a claim that what we think of as personality draws only on gender stereotypes, nor that children or indeed adults gravitate only towards characteristics socially coded as corresponding with their sex. The problem arises that if we train children to think in terms of stereotypes, nonconformity may be interpreted as evidence of incongruence with their sex category, leading to children being encouraged to think of themselves as actually being a girl or a boy depending on that characteristic or stereotype, rather than their body. Nevertheless, it is important to remember that we don't know the role that self-image plays in the absorbing of stereotypes – that is to say, we don't know to what extent transitioning as a young person affects the gender messaging they receive. It could be, and has been, argued that the younger a person socially transitions, the less of their life they spend exposed to the sex-role stereotypes projected upon them by others who do not know their sex and therefore absorbing the lessons of their prescribed gender. It is also argued that the earlier they transition medically (particularly hormonally), the less their bodies develop physically along the paths dictated by their biology. It could be that this group of people are more likely to 'pass' than others. It is also true that some people develop naturally (I'm not talking about genitals but in terms of height, shoulder size/ shape, body shape, foot and hand size, facial characteristics) with physical characteristics more similar to those associated with the opposite sex. These people may also pass most of the time. Nevertheless, post-puberty transition arguably does greatly limit someone's chance of passing, and extensive surgery and treatment is prohibitively expensive for many, while socially constructed and learned gendered behaviours also play a role in determining whether someone is publicly accepted as passing: women are, famously, conditioned to be kind at the cost of honesty, comfort or even their own safety.

It is perhaps more useful to use the term 'gender affirmation surgery' than 'sex change' and frame our understanding as such; however, this understanding of the value of gender affirmation surgery to some who undergo it cannot come at the cost of replacing sex with gender identity as a primary way to categorise people.[29] Neither should the benign sounding 'gender affirmation' be allowed to disguise the brutal and painful reality of penectomy and orchidectomy (removal of penis and scrotum), oophorectomy and hysterectomy (removal of ovaries and uterus), phalloplasty and scrotoplasty (construction of a phallus and scrotum using skin usually taken from the arm), metoidioplasty (creation of a phallus from a hormonally enlarged clitoris) and mastectomy (removal of the breasts) or the irreversible nature of some hormone treatments.[30,31] The 'treatments' undertaken vary significantly and include surgery, hormones and voice and behaviour modification. Most males who say they have transitioned still have a penis, regardless of whether or not they have obtained a Gender Recognition Certificate. Research estimates prevalence rates of genital surgery in males with transgender identities as being 5–10 per cent; in other words, 90–95 per cent still have a penis.[32,33,34] Youth, poverty and belonging to a minoritised racial group are negative correlates; in other words, transitioning older white males with higher incomes are more likely to have genital surgery.[35]

Some make a point of retaining characteristics associated with their sex whilst claiming to belong to the opposite category, including Alex Drummond, who has had no surgery and retains a full beard. Drummond claimed, 'I identify as lesbian as I'm female' and 'I'm widening the bandwidth of how to be a woman'.[36] Remaining visible as transgender can be a political choice – a refusal to conform – with those who attempt to pass labelled 'assimilationist'.[37] For others, the idea of passing is important to their belief in being able to live authentically or safely.[38] However, 'the choice to "pass" is a privilege that is only available to trans people who are able to "pass"'[39] and using a transgender person's visibility as an excuse for violence or abuse is unacceptable. Speaking out against the pressure to pass or judging those who do not, transgender activist Eva Echo said, 'We shouldn't be moulding ourselves to fit society. Society needs to make room for us – accepting us as we are.'[40] I agree with Eva Echo's words but not the sentiment. Transgender people should be accepted as they are, but not as the sex that they are not.

One often hears the accusation 'you're denying my existence' from trans rights activists. Disagreeing with the beliefs of someone is not the same as saying that they don't exist. Many people use social descriptors in our ideas about who we are; we're talking about someone's internal idea of themselves, such as feminist, vegan or sky diver. These are things we do, or believe about ourselves. It doesn't matter what anyone else thinks. Nevertheless, I believe sex influences a person's experience of the world in numerous important ways and I don't believe that people can change sex. Some people, however, believe that they can, and legally, birth certificates and other documents can be changed as if this were true. Others confuse or conflate sex and gender, and believe or say that they believe that people can change from one category to another. We're all still female or male, regardless of the choices that we make and ways we live our lives. Does this mean that transition cannot be meaningful? Not necessarily, but I would prefer that there was more interest in changing society by dismantling the system of gender, rather than changing bodies. For some, however, it appears that transition can be meaningful for the person concerned and those they are connected to, in both positive and negative ways.[41] But problems arise when the consequences of that transition are imposed on other people.

The true trans fallacy, like the true Scotsman fallacy, is used when people attempt to defend a claim by excluding any examples that do not fit the picture that they are trying to create. So, males with transgender identities who exist at the extreme end of the scale of exploitative, abusive or violent males, are written off by trans rights activists as 'not really trans', despite the broad definition of trans suggested by the charity which describes itself as standing 'for lesbian, gay, bi, trans, queer, questioning and ace (LGBTQ+) people everywhere' – Stonewall – in their list of LGBTQ+ terms into which they almost all clearly fit.[42] This fallacy is a linguistic tool that functions to maintain boundaries and construct unchallengeable arguments.

The existence of intersex people (now increasingly and more accurately termed 'people with differences in sex development', or DSDs) has been used by some to try to make the claim that it is wrong to say that there are two sexes: female and male; or as a kind of 'gotcha' to catch out those who advocate for single-sex spaces. Briefly, people with DSDs have been born with some medical conditions which affect reproductive functioning. This doesn't mean that they're on some mid-point between the sexes. People with DSDs are still either female or male. They are not 'proof that sex is a spectrum'.[43,44]

And non-binary? Non-binary people prefer not to be thought of as belonging to either category of 'woman' or 'man', but as with all humans, in reality, they are still one or the other sex, and are affected by this like everyone else. At best, non-binary identity is just a different way of saying that they don't wish to conform to the stereotypes associated with their sex. At worst, it's an indirect way of saying that they, unlike most other people, have managed to transcend that which most of us fail to do, and consigns all those not designated non-binary to the land of sex-role stereotypes.

I recognise that people who identify as transgender can face transphobia: discrimination, violence and abuse.[45] Of course, I do not think that is acceptable. However, it is not transphobic, in my opinion, to believe that people cannot change sex, that women's oppression is based on our sex, and that gender is a hierarchy. Sex is the axis of sex-based oppression and gender is the biggest tool in the box. Feminism is ultimately optimistic and offers the hope of change and a better world. This book does not argue that all biological males, whether or not they have transgender identities, are predators and abusers.

I have spent more than three decades working with and for women who have been subjected to men's violence, in London and West Yorkshire. I did this first as a support worker in a hostel for homeless women and then in a women's refuge. After about five years, I got my first job as a manager, but for

most of the next decade I worked for small charities, still based
inside the refuge or women's hostel. In my working life I have
focused on supporting women, but I have always understood
that work to be political.

I joined a charity called nia as their Chief Executive in 2009.
nia supports women, girls and children who have been subjected to sexual and domestic violence and abuse, including
prostitution. We at nia understand that the ways in which
men abuse women can't be divided into boxes; there are
overlaps between all these forms of violence, abuse and violations, and our work reflects this. We run specialist refuges for
women with problematic substance use and also for women
escaping sexual exploitation as well as a range of community-
based services. We support over 2,000 women and girls every
year.

Many charities, especially those providing services, lose
their political edge. Not nia. We see defending women's sex-
based rights as absolutely integral to what we do. As far as I
know, nia was the first UK organisation to actively and openly
defend single-sex spaces for victims-survivors of men's violence. I have been aware of the growing threat to single-sex
services for a long time. Unfortunately, sometimes being Chief
Executive of a charity means keeping your mouth shut, and
for a while that's what nia's trustees asked of me. In 2017,
however, the trustees agreed that we would make the defence
of single-sex services a strategic priority. We – the board and
senior management team of nia – knew this was a risk to the
charity's survival and that it might attract negative attention,
but we agreed that inaction meant we would be complicit in
the erasure of single-sex services, so we decided that we'd face
the risk. In short, if this was going to bring about the end of nia,
it was the hill we were prepared to die on and that we'd do so
proudly knowing that we were doing what we were supposed
to do: protecting women, girls and children who have been
subjected to men's violence.

In 2019, I gave evidence in parliament to the WESC about how the Equality Act 2010 affects the operation of single-sex services for women who'd been subjected to men's violence. Towards the end of the session, the representative of Women's Aid Federation England (WAFE), the national umbrella charity working to end domestic abuse against women and children, claimed that services for women who had survived men's violence had been developed, not based only on biology but on an understanding of how patriarchy operates too.[46] Whilst this is in some respects true, I don't believe that this understanding attempted to deny the links between biological sex and patterns in the perpetration of, or victimisation in, domestic violence and abuse.

In addition to my job at nia, I research, and campaign on femicide/men's fatal violence against women.[47] I started looking at femicide in January 2012 following the murder of a young woman who had been referred to nia a few weeks earlier, Kirsty Treloar. When I searched for information about what had happened to her, I came across so many reports of women who'd been killed by men since the start of the year, that I made a list of their names so that I could figure out how many there were. In the first three days of 2012, eight women in the UK were killed by men. This observation became a project that I called 'Counting Dead Women'. Just over a year later, Clarrie O'Callaghan and I had a conversation that eventually led to the development of the Femicide Census, a unique comprehensive record and analysis of all women killed by men in the UK since 2009. I've submitted a thesis for a PhD in the subject and hope to graduate in 2023.

I grew up in an economically comfortable working-class family in a village outside a mill town in the North of England. The decline of the woollen industry in the 1980s, like the decline of mining, textiles and manufacturing in other parts of the North and Midlands, meant that the day-to-day lives of ordinary people went through a massive change in a generation. I genuinely couldn't see how my life could have more in common with those I saw as 'posh girls' whom I'd met at sixth form college, compared with the lads who lived in my street who I hung out with in my early teens. I was social-class conscious before I was sex-class conscious and this continues to shape my feminism. This predated Kimberlé Crenshaw's work on intersectionality and the understanding that different forms of structural inequality, discrimination, and hate can overlap and compound one another,[48] but 'A' level sociology at least eventually provided a link to socialist feminism. Ironically, although the concept of intersectional feminism is now more widely understood, I think that social class has become one of the least well-understood inequalities. Being working class almost always means that less is expected of and available to you, having lower aspirations, settling for less and certainly being judged as less. It is absolutely right that feminism integrates resistance to other forms of oppression and subjugation – race, class, disability, sexuality and so on – insofar as they affect women. But, at no point does being male intersect with or compound the experience of a female. Including males in the concept of intersectionality would change the definition of the term. Lose the structural analysis and feminism gets lost in the rights of the individual, in identity-led politics and notions of choice and agency, which fail to take sufficient account of power, context and impact. In my view, the focus and priority of feminism should always be women. Feminism is the fight for the liberation of all women as a class from subjugation under patriarchy.

Men's violence against women crosses boundaries of class, race and age, but it is working-class women of all ethnic groups who have fewest options. The issue of single-sex spaces for women who have been subjected to men's violence is a class issue. And it is also a racial, cultural and religious issue, in so far as racial, religious and cultural differences can overlap. For example, some women from minoritised or marginalised groups are prohibited by their religions from entering mixed-sex spaces in some circumstances.

Although I was too young to have been at risk as a victim, growing up in Yorkshire in the 1970s and 1980s meant growing up under the shadow of Peter Sutcliffe. I was 7 when he killed 28-year-old Wilma McCann, as far as we know, his first murder victim; 12 when he killed his last. He was charged in 1981 – when I was a few weeks shy of 13 – for murdering 13 women in less than 6 years. It's no exaggeration to say that his violence was a formative influence. The murders of five children by Ian Brady and Myra Hindley had happened shortly before I was born (between 1963 and 1965), yet contributed to an almost tangible feeling in Lancashire and Yorkshire that danger was out there. On a more personal level, there was men's violence against women in my family, friends' families and friends' relationships, and like many young women I had direct experiences of male sexual violence. But without a feminist analysis, I had no concept of this as part of a continuum of male violence that functions to control and restrict all women. I was surrounded by men's violence but unable to see it or make the connections.

In this book we are going to journey through sex inequality, and particularly men's violence against women and girls, look at how specialist services for women victim-survivors were developed and why they were needed, pausing to look at how the funding of those services created conditions which discouraged feminist political approaches. I'll look at some of the issues outside services for women who've been subjected to sexual and domestic violence and abuse, and how gender identity ideology and transgender activism has threatened women-only, that is single-sex, spaces. And I will look at and celebrate women's resistance.

Most people, fortunately, have not been subjected to violence and abuse and do not need specialist single-sex services. Many women, however, want single-sex toilets and changing rooms, or can see the unfairness of the inclusion of males in female sport; and even if they themselves have never been abused, many women can empathise with those who have and recognise that they may need single-sex space for recovery. I will not sit back and let those who do not need or want single-sex services take them away from those who do.

2

Sex Inequality

What's men's violence against women and girls got to do with it?

Women have not been given equal rights. We have had to fight every step of the way. The right of married women to own and control their own property (not only buildings but personal possessions too) and earnings was secured after years of campaigning by women's groups, in the Married Women's Property Act 1870. This bill was passed by a parliament entirely composed of men because women were prohibited from voting and becoming MPs. After decades of campaigning, the right of some women, not all, to vote in national elections was finally won in 1918. In the same year, the first woman MP, Constance Markiewicz, was elected to the House of Commons.[1] She did not take her seat, declining it from prison in Dublin, as did other Sinn Fein politicians, who refused to swear an oath of allegiance to the king and becoming a member of the newly created Dáil Éireann, the Irish parliament, instead. A year later, in the Plymouth Sutton by-election, Nancy Astor was elected for the Conservative Party and became the first female sitting MP.[2] A decade after the election of Markiewicz, in 1928, 61 years after the formation of The London Society for Women's Suffrage, women finally gained the same voting rights as men.

Much more recently, in 1982, journalist Anna Coote and solicitor Tess Gill had to take to the law for their right, as women, to be served in the El Vino bar on Fleet Street.[3] Their landmark case made clear that excuses of courtesy, propriety or chivalry were not legally permissible defences for sex discrimination. In 1973, in *Director of Public Prosecutions (DPP) v. Morgan*, Morgan told three of his friends that his wife was 'kinky' and set them up to rape her. He did not frame the planned acts as non-consensual; indeed, the three friends claimed that Morgan told them to ignore her if she resisted as feigning protest was part of the 'game'. They were found guilty of rape, though received derisory sentences. Morgan was found not guilty of rape but of aiding and abetting because being married to the victim meant he could not have raped her; in other words, marriage was an accepted absolute defence for rape in the English court of law.[4] This remained the case until *R v. R* in 1991 when a man was convicted of attempting to rape his wife.[5] It wasn't until 2018 that women in Ireland had the right to have an abortion on request until the twelfth week of pregnancy.[6] Yet rights won can be taken away. Women's right to an abortion was secured in the USA in 1973 in a case known as *Roe v. Wade*, but in Texas, in 2021, almost all abortions – after foetal cardiac activity can be detected, occurring around the sixth week of pregnancy, which for many women might be before they're even aware that they are pregnant – were banned. In 2022, the US Supreme Court overturned abortion as a woman's constitutional right, meaning that states could legislate individually. Within weeks, nine states had implemented trigger laws banning abortion after six weeks of pregnancy unless necessary to save the life of the pregnant woman. A further four states had abortion bans in progress and eight states had attempted to ban the procedure but had been blocked by the courts from doing so.[7]

It is almost half a century since the UK parliament passed the Sex Discrimination Act in 1975, which thirty-five years later, in 2010, was replaced by the Equality Act.[8] The Equality Act brought together and replaced existing equalities legislation from different areas and is intended to protect people from discrimination in employment and wider aspects of life. It identified nine 'protected characteristics': age, disability, marriage/civil partnership, pregnancy/maternity, race, religion/belief, sexual orientation, gender reassignment and sex. This book will be looking at some of the tensions between the last two: gender reassignment and sex.

For many feminists, me included, there is a question of whether equality between women and men is possible, or even desirable in today's society. Of course, we want equal pay for work of equal value, but we also need to look at how and why some occupations or tasks are deemed to be more valuable than others and why greater value is so often assigned to work mainly undertaken by men. Work has no inherent value and just somehow, we've ended up with women's work being undervalued. So, unless we all do more of the same, or unless we increase the value of what we see as 'women's work', we're stuck. Wage equality without radical reform is an impossible dream.

We don't want to see men sexually objectified, flaunting their curves and squeezing their feet into shoes that they kick off before hitting the dancefloor; what we want is an end to misogynistic beauty standards and practices.

We don't want women to be paying for sexual access to the bodies of men who have too few choices; we want an end to prostitution and that requires economic security for all. It is not possible to have sexual equality for all in a society when one sex is the one that is for sale – a commodity or service – and the other sex is the consumer, and almost always the purveyor (pimp); consumers have rights over and above the goods and services that they buy. Legalising prostitution isn't the answer either. Women who have exited prostitution in Germany and New Zealand, where the purchasing of sex was decriminalised and prostitution became regulated by the state, said that things got worse, not better after decriminalisation, for example, with brothel owners competing to offer the lowest prices and bargains to feed increased demand and attract the emboldened men who could shop around with impunity.[9,10]

Of course, we want everyone to be equal under the law, but the law was mainly written by powerful and wealthy white men and still serves the interests of the same group. One of the most fundamental premises of UK law – 'innocent until proven guilty' – stacks the system against victims of sexual and many other crimes of violence and abuse because lack of evidence is synonymous with innocence.[11]

It is in men's violence against women that we see some of the most horrific manifestations of sex inequality. Sex differences in victimisation and perpetration of sexual and domestic violence are unequivocal. As we saw in chapter 1, for the year ending March 2020, according to the Office for National Statistics (ONS), 74 per cent of all victims of recorded domestic abuse-related offences against adults aged between 16 and 74 years were female. This breaks down to women being 74 per cent of domestic abuse-related victims of criminal damage and arson, 77 per cent of victims of public order offences, 73 per cent of victims of crimes against the person, 94 per cent of domestic abuse-related sexual offences,[12] and 83 per cent of victims of high frequency repeat crimes (more than 10 crimes) are women.[13] Males constituted 92 per cent of defendants in domestic abuse-related prosecutions in England and Wales in the year ending March 2020,[14] and 98 per cent of perpetrators of rapes and assaults by penetration in England and Wales were males.[15] It is estimated that approximately 72,800 people are involved in prostitution in the UK, and that 88 per cent are female.[16] Girls are at least three times more likely than boys to report experiences of child sexual abuse.[17]

It isn't just the rates of sexual and domestic violence perpetration and victimisation that are different; sexual and domestic violence have different impacts on women and men. Women suffer greater fear of the partner who is abusing them.[18] When I talk about sex differences and reporting of domestic and sexual violence, people often suggest that the differences are exaggerated because it's such a taboo for men to report. Not only does this fail to recognise that reporting abuse is also a taboo for many women, but research has found the opposite to be true: that men overestimate their victimisation and underestimate their own violence, whereas women are more likely to overestimate their own use of violence but underestimate their victimisation. Women normalise, discount, minimise, excuse their partners' domestic and sexual violence against them, and they're more likely to find ways to make it their fault.[19] Another piece of research found that when women were reported to the police for abuse, which men often do as a form of attack, they (women) were arrested to a disproportionate degree given the fewer incidents where they were perpetrators. The study found that men were arrested for one in every ten incidents, whilst women were arrested for one in every three incidents.[20]

People can be incredibly resistant to considering facts that don't fit with their world view and the belief that women are as violent and abusive as men is one that too many seem to be unwilling to let go of. Sex differences in intimate partner homicide rates (homicide includes killings sentenced as both murders and manslaughters) show that so-called 'sex symmetry' is a myth. In England and Wales in the 11 years from April 2009 to March 2020, 1,027 people were killed by a current or former partner; 890 (87 per cent) of the victims were female, 137 (13 per cent) were male, and 89 per cent of perpetrators were male.[21] Looking beyond intimate partner homicide to all homicides, there were a total of 6,568 victims of homicide in England and Wales for the 11 years ending March 2020, of which 32 per cent of victims were female and 68 per cent male. Of 6,324 homicide indictments (charges), 9 per cent of the suspects were female and 91 per cent percent were male.[22] You also see different relationships between killers and their victims according to the sex of the victim. Women are most likely to be killed by a partner or ex-partner. In the UK, again, according to the ONS, about half (49 per cent) of women homicide victims are killed by a partner or ex-partner. The Femicide Census, looking at cases where a man has been charged with a woman's murder, found that figure to be around 62 per cent, and 12–15 per cent are killed by other family members. In total, according to the ONS, 73 per cent of women murder victims are killed by someone they know, whereas for men it is 48 per cent. Roughly 10 per cent of women victims are killed by a stranger; for men that figure is 27 per cent. Only 3.3 per cent of all men murdered are killed by a current or former partner and 5.1 per cent by another family member.[23]

If you look at what women and men do to inflict fatal injuries, that's different too. The Femicide Census has analysed men's fatal violence in the UK since 2009, including methods used to kill. In our 10-year report on femicides between 2009 and 2018, we found that a sharp instrument was used in 30 per cent of cases where men killed women, strangulation in 13 per cent of cases, a blunt instrument in 11 per cent of cases and hitting, kicking, stamping and bashing without a weapon in 9 per cent of cases. There isn't directly comparable data for what women do when they kill, but the Centre for Women's Justice (CWJ) researched women who kill male partners. They found that 108 men had been killed by female partners between April 2008 and March 2018, in comparison to 840 women killed by male current/former partners in the same time period. CWJ collected data on 92 of these cases and found that women who killed male partners were more likely than men who killed female partners to use a weapon, stabbing him in 71 per cent of cases, and in 9 per cent of cases another type of weapon was used. Only one woman strangled her current/former partner. Men are able to use strangulation, hitting and kicking – in other words, the force and strength of their bodies – to kill a woman because they are generally bigger and physically stronger.[24]

There is a further important difference. The Femicide Census found evidence in 59 per cent of cases that the man who killed a female partner or ex-partner had been violent and/or abusive to them in the past. This is highly likely to be an undercount since it is not unusual for women to tell no one that they are being abused, and also in many cases, this might not have been reported in publicly available information even if someone did know about it. CWJ found a very different picture: in 77 per cent of cases, men killed by their female partners had been abusing these women prior to the murder.[25]

Finally, men who are killed by current or former partners are significantly more likely than women to be killed by someone of the same sex. Using the ONS data I mentioned earlier for homicides in the 11 years ending March 2020, of 137 male victims, 109 were killed by women (79 per cent). Of 890 female victims, 884 (99 per cent) were killed by men. There were 912 men who killed a current or former partner and 115 women. So, one in five men (20.4 per cent) killed by a current or former partner were killed by a man; for women, approximately one in 147 women killed by a current or former partner were killed by a woman. Men who are killed by a current or former partner are therefore 29 times more likely to be killed by someone of the same sex than women are.

It is important that we recognise the overlaps between sexual and domestic violence and abuse, and other forms of men's violence against women such as prostitution. Policy and legislation have created divisions that all too often do not reflect the realities of women's lives. Many women are subjected to sexual violence, abuse, humiliation and degradation by the men who are supposed to love them. Most child sex abuse is committed by men in the family. Many young women and girls are groomed into prostitution by someone that they thought was a boyfriend, who little by little becomes their pimp or both. Feminist academic Liz Kelly talked about 'the continuum of sexual violence' to describe how all these forms of violence and others, such as street harassment, are linked.[26] It is useful and necessary to be able to distinguish between different forms of men's violence and abuse; however, if they are taken outside the context of men's violence against women, terms like domestic violence and sexual abuse also blur the reality of overlaps and can create a false sex neutrality. This hides differences between sexes, that are even there when we look at something like killing. The term gender-based violence is the same. Recognising the role of socially created gender is useful, whilst neglecting to name the male agent is a form of patriarchal censorship. We need to use terms like domestic violence, sexual abuse and gender-based violence with caution.

Men's violence against women is a global issue and affects women from all ethnic groups. In the UK, there is evidence to suggest that Black, Asian and mixed heritage women may be more at risk of some forms of abuse and face additional barriers, including (but not limited to) racism when accessing support.[27] Writing about women from minoritised ethnic groups, Hannana Siddiqui said that it is important to recognise 'similarity and difference between BME and white majority women', avoiding both denial of the specificity of minoritised women's experiences, and failing to recognise the commonalities.[28] Arguments that focus on culture as a contributor often ignore that many who are equally embedded in the same culture are not violent, and that men in any culture exercise choice when they abuse women and children; also, that there are harmful practices across all cultures but many are less inclined to identify the cultural forces that influence violence and abuse in their own groups. Others have made links between blaming intimate partner killings on women's infidelity and so-called 'honour'-based violence.[29]

Researchers have compared measures of sex inequality and

rates of men's violence against women in different countries and found that, in general, the higher the level of sex equality, the lower the level of men's violence against women. However, they have also identified something called the 'Nordic paradox', where there are higher levels of reported sexual and domestic violence and abuse reported by women in Sweden, Finland and Denmark, three of the countries with the highest levels of economic, employment, power and health equality.[30] The researchers were not able to explain this but hypothesised that it could be down to a backlash against women, increased conflict because of increased equality, the clash of individually held sexist beliefs and egalitarian social norms, and women being more likely to report violence and abuse as a result of decreased inequality and a societally agreed condemnation of men's violence against women.

Recognising sex differences in violence, in perpetration and victimisation, in what is done to whom and by whom, and concluding that women are disproportionately victimised by men and that men are hugely disproportionately the perpetrators, is not the same as saying that we don't care about male victims. Nor is it the same as saying that we don't think women can be abusive or violent. But I am saying that sex differences in violence reflect sex inequality and that if we want to do something about one or the other, we need to address both. Women will continue to lose out if we ignore sex differences.

Where do people with a trans identity fit into sex differences and violence? More critically, for this book, where do males who identify as transwomen or even who identify as women fit in? Is it transphobic to talk about men's violence? Does self-image and the desire to be identified as a woman reliably impact on a male's likelihood of violent offending? Is it transphobic to draw conclusions about males who identify as transgender from data about males? One of the first things to say is that we do not have any data to make a case for any other position. The number of people who identify as transgender has increased hugely over the last decade and there is no reliable count even of the population. In 2018, the government estimated that there are 200,000–500,000 trans people in the UK, while Stonewall estimate that possibly 1 per cent (600,000) of the UK population identify as transgender or non-binary.[31] Other research has estimated between 0.39 and 2 per cent of the global population could be counted as transgender, non-binary or some other related classification.[32,33,34] So, we don't even know how many people identify as transgender, let alone know the proportion of females or males within this number who commit or are subjected to violent crime.

The best data we currently have on transgender males and their rates of committing violent crime is an academically rigorous study published in Sweden in 2011, which looked at social and health outcomes for people who had surgically, hormonally and legally undergone transition and compared them to a matched control group of people of their birth sex.[35] Their study of 324 people was split into two groups, those transitioning between 1973 and 1988 and those transitioning between 1989 and 2003. Those in the latter group had received mental health support as well as hormones and surgery. They found that those in the earlier group were more likely to commit violent crime than those of their birth sex in the control group and that those in the second group committed crime in line with people of their birth sex. In other words, criminal behaviours of those who had legally and medically transitioned from men to transwomen followed the pattern of male offending and those who had transitioned from women to transmen continued with female pattern offending. Males who had transitioned were 18 times more likely to be convicted of violent crime than females. Some transgender rights activists claim that the study's authors themselves have since discredited the findings, but a closer look at the claims found that denials came about because others were drawing conclusions which the study's findings did not support.

It is also important to recognise that the subjects of this research had undergone surgical and hormonal treatment, as well as legal changes. This means that they were a much more strictly defined group than those who might simply self-define, declare or who would claim to be gender-fluid or non-binary. Policy analysts Murray Blackburn Mackenzie conducted a careful analysis of the research and demonstrated that it had not been debunked at all.[36] In short, the study's finding held true: that with regard to violent offending, birth sex matters.

We should be able to go to Stonewall for accurate data in the UK, but I don't think their data is reliable enough. Data on hate crimes against people who are transgender can include people not using preferred pronouns, preventing them from transitioning or referring to their actual sex instead of their chosen gender identity. We simply don't have reliable information about the violence and abuse that people who identify as transgender are subjected to. It is not clear whether the people who lose most from this are those who identify as transgender or women: transgender people because we are prevented from developing services to match need and demand because the claims being made are unreliable and patchy; or women, because policy-makers accept inflated claims about the risk of abuse suffered by people who identify as transgender and underestimate the victimisation of women.[37]

Transgender Trend, an organisation of parents, professionals and academics based in the UK who are concerned about the current approach to diagnosis of children as transgender, and Fair Play for Women found that Stonewall and Mermaids (an organisation founded to support – enable and encourage affirmative approaches for – young trans people and their families) were making misleading claims about the risks of suicide in young people who self-identified as transgender.[38,39]

Sex remains a major and structural axis of inequality. For sure, it is not the only one. Global capitalism creates and maintains the inequities of the geopolitical north and south and huge wealth disparities within countries. Racism remains institutional and systemic. Sex is the biological group into which we are born and in which we remain. Men's violence against women and girls is both a cause and consequence of sex inequality and gender is one of the critical ways in which men's violence is created, normalised and frequently excused. Sex inequality still exists. Sex still matters. It is hubris to act as if we exist in a post-sex society, and doing so means women lose out. The best trick patriarchy ever played is convincing most people that it does not exist, but feminists recognise patriarchy and highlight sex inequality and its profound damages.

3

Standing on the Shoulders of Giants

Men's violence against women gained attention as a serious issue in activism and the academy in the late 1960s and 1970s, and was a key tenet of second-wave feminism. Later, the cumulative impact of women's sustained efforts began to change statutory services, the law and politics. In this chapter I will look at how women, feminist activists and survivors, many women being both, developed the responses to men's violence against women and girls. I will also ask how this movement lost its power and its nerve.

Gill Hague has written a book chronicling the UK development of specialist services for women who have been subjected to men's violence.[1] She makes links between what was happening in the UK, with parallel developments, not just in the West, in Europe, the USA and Canada, but in the Global South and East. She identified the anti-Vietnam movement, the peace and left movements, civil rights, and Black Power as the foundations for the women's liberation movement, as women in these movements recognised and were dissatisfied that their voices were being overlooked and silenced. Feminism is not a single-issue movement and it is important to recognise that for many women, their class, their race, their socialism, pacifism

and anti-colonialism were always indivisible from their feminism. It is important to recognise that whilst Black, Asian and
women from other minoritised ethnic groups, and working-
class women were active participants in these movements
– contributing, raising intersecting issues and developing their
own responses – they were also often simultaneously marginalised and their concerns overlooked. Any contemporaneous
movement needs to find the balance between its responsibility
to recognise and avoid xenophobia, ignorance of class and race
advantages and disadvantages and to make sure that when we
look back to the movements which preceded us, we do not
make invisible the contributions of marginalised and minoritised women who went before.[2]

Second-wave feminists were mostly from the generation
known as the baby-boomers who benefitted from a mas-
sively expanded welfare state, in particular free at the point
of delivery education and healthcare. I was born in 1968, and
it's hard for me to imagine the restrictions on life that I have
avoided because I was able to take for granted free contra-
ception and education. For those born since the millennium,
for whom almost an incalculable body of information (and
misinformation) is available at the touch of a finger, it must be
inconceivable to think that in the 1960s, women who we now
know as feminist luminaries, were tentatively discovering and
naming their shared sex-based oppression without the huge
canon of thought so easily accessible to us now.

Hague cites Jalna Hamner, an incredible feminist activist
and academic, talking about participating in consciousness-
raising groups, which were the cornerstones of the women's
liberation movement:

> . . . women *didn't* understand why they felt so bad, they couldn't
> see why. . . . They *didn't* understand why they couldn't do the
> things they wanted to do. It was just a kind of terrible mystery.
> So it was only by talking about it that there began to be some

understanding. And it was really understanding about oppression. And where did the oppression come from. And who is oppressing me. And how this can be overcome.[3]

I've addressed the development of the women's liberation movement, the second wave, because it was from this movement and in this context that the movement identifying, naming, resisting and responding to men's violence against women, girls and children grew. Women – feminist activists and victim-survivors – knew that you were not one or the other, like today, many women are both. It wasn't unusual for women who stayed in refuges to become volunteers or take up paid employment in them when they left. I know several leaders, Directors or Chief Executives of domestic violence services who were once women contacting that service for support. Feminist politics and an understanding of the role of men's violence against women in patriarchal societies was integral to how services were developed and support was delivered.

The 1970s saw women's refuges and services for women who had been subjected to sexual violence opening across the country. This was truly a grassroots movement. The services were developed and run by women on the ground, often with very little, if any funding, little experience of providing support outside friends and family and without government backing. London Rape Crisis was set up in 1976, so too was the first Rape Crisis service in Scotland, in Glasgow.[4] Community-based services for women who had been subjected to men's violence were developed, in many cases subsequently, sometimes by groups running refuges, sometimes independently of them. In some towns and cities women developed support services for women involved in prostitution. It is widely believed that the first refuge for women fleeing violent male partners in the UK and possibly the world was opened in west London in 1971, by Chiswick Women's Aid, led by Erin Pizzey and Anne Ashby. Anne Ashby (1938–2005) is much less widely known than Erin

Pizzey, but her contribution should not be forgotten. Erin was the frontwoman, the voice of the organisation, but Anne's contribution was essential to founding the refuge and keeping it running. I was fortunate enough to know Anne when I was a Refuge Worker for Westminster Women's Aid from 1992 to 1995. She was a management committee member. It was around this time that many women's refuges and other organisations stopped running as collectives (where in theory at least, though much more rarely in practice, everyone had equal status) and reformed as hierarchies with decision-making and responsibility structures, and sought the status of registered charities. nia, the organisation I currently work for, followed a similar trajectory. It began as Hackney Women's Aid in 1975, became a charity in 1991 and became the nia project, to reflect its broader approach addressing all forms of men's violence against women, in 2003. I joined as Chief Executive in 2009.

It is not only in services specifically addressing the needs of victim-survivors of men's violence where single-sex services have been developed. Though arguably, to a greater or lesser degree, women need these other services because of the abuse they have suffered from men or the ongoing threat of predatory and/or abusive men. Homelessness services, including hostels, were largely developed for men, based on men's needs. Women who are homeless are less visible amongst those who are street homeless and more likely to double up with friends or family or find other forms of temporary, insecure and usually low-quality accommodation.[5] According to the homeless charity Shelter, in the last 10 years, the number of women in England who are homeless and living in temporary accommodation has increased by 88 per cent.[6] Drug and alcohol support services are very rarely women-only, despite the high prevalence of women, who have been subjected to or are still living with men's violence and abuse, accessing them, though some may offer women-only sessions. Through my work on men's fatal violence against women, I have seen a number of cases where women have been befriended by men with histories of violence and abuse while accessing drug and alcohol services, and who have later been killed by those men. Whether or not men were consciously using the services to access vulnerable women is beside the point – the lack of woman-only support placed these women at risk.

The need for women-only space – for the dignity and safety of women – had been recognised well before the 1970s. Millbank Prison, established in 1816, was the first modern state prison in England to (briefly) hold only women. Built in 1852, Holloway Prison was mixed sex and became a women-only prison in 1903, the first suffragette arriving in 1906. The UK's earliest public toilets began to appear in the mid-nineteenth century, with the first public flushing toilet in the Great Exhibition at the Crystal Palace in Hyde Park, London, in 1851. The lack of public toilets affected women's ability to participate in public life to the extent that the phrase 'urinary leash' was used to refer to the restriction of women's movements. In the mid-1850s, the Ladies Sanitary Association began campaigning for women's public toilets and later the Union of Women's Liberal and Radical Associations campaigned in Camden, London, for toilets for working-class women, with initial plans held back several years by men objecting to the toilets being located next to their own.

One of the main successes of feminism has been getting men's violence against women, girls and children on to the mainstream policy agenda, but this has come at a cost. The price we have paid is depoliticisation – specifically, watering down of feminist politics. In 2021, the UK government released the third national strategy to tackle violence against women and girls. Separately, the Domestic Abuse Bill was signed into law, becoming the Domestic Abuse Act. The Domestic Abuse Act therefore carries more weight than the strategy. The Act has what the Home Office describes as a 'gender-neutral' definition of domestic abuse. This means that the UK's most significant piece of legislation addressing possibly the most prevalent form of men's violence against women has been taken outside the context of men's violence against women. In addition, the Act does not offer equal protection to migrant women with insecure immigration status, despite the concerted efforts of feminists to rectify this as the Bill was being processed.

The Istanbul Convention is an international framework, which, 10 years after signing, in 2012, the UK still had not ratified; in other words it hasn't turned the steps outlined in the treaty into actions. The treaty is clear:

> ... violence against women is a manifestation of historically unequal power relations between women and men, which have led to domination over, and discrimination against, women by men and to the prevention of the full advancement of women ... Recognising the structural nature of violence against women as gender-based violence, and that violence against women is one of the crucial social mechanisms by which women are forced into a subordinate position compared with men.[7]

There are several areas where the UK government falls short of the requirements of the Istanbul Convention, which arguably may explain the failure to ratify. For instance, the Convention requires member states to provide support and financial resources to civil society organisations working to prevent and combat all forms of male violence against women. The UK government has produced several reports on its progress towards ratifying the Istanbul Convention, which present the Domestic Abuse Act as the vehicle to ensure that UK domestic legislation is compliant with the Istanbul Convention. The most recent government report in 2020 recognises that the UK government currently falls short of Article 4(3) of the treaty, which relates to non-discrimination, due to the way migrant women are disadvantaged when trying to access services.

The Istanbul Convention recognises that violence against women is a manifestation of 'historically' unequal power relations between men and women. 'Historically' could imply that this inequality does not remain – and, like the UK government's strategy, shies away from what could be a powerful step – naming men as the agent of that violence in the title of any legislative framework.

These are key national and international tools to address men's violence against women but for them to have become such, feminist ground has been ceded: naming men as the agent, connecting all forms of men's violence against women within a framework which recognises patriarchy, and offering equal protection to all women. The issue is not that the legislation so far is unhelpful or even that it does not represent huge steps forward, but that it fails to live up to what we would seek with truly feminist legislation, which at the very least would fully link sex inequality and men's violence against women and apply equally to all women. For me, it would also need to aim to abolish prostitution and seriously address the objectification of women and sex-role stereotypes; that is, socially constructed gender.

I want to look now at the development of funding for women's refuges and how that changed in the twenty-first century and the serious effect this has had.

Under Tony Blair's New Labour government, a programme was introduced in 2003 called 'Supporting People' (SP). It created a £1.8 billion ring-fenced grant to local authorities intended to fund services to help vulnerable people live independently. Funding for women's refuges was a specified part of this grant. It made an absolutely fundamental change to the way organisations running women's refuges and homelessness hostels were funded.

At that time, there were lots of very small independent local charities running domestic violence refuges and this landscape was very different from today's. Since their development in the 1970s, many of these charities received some form of local authority funding. How much and how it was administered varied from place to place. There was a national target that each local authority should have access to one refuge space per 10,000 of their local population, though many places fell short of this. Under SP, a standardised funding formula was introduced, though in reality how it was interpreted varied a lot, and an unprecedented level of funding security was promised. However, with this new funding, the model of funding was changed and grants were replaced by contracts commissioned by local authorities. The importance of this came to light in later years. The programme included the foundations for a move to open competitive tendering. From thereon in, the little grants to local charities across the country were advertised as pots of funding for specified services that any organisation, provided they could demonstrate the necessary level of quality (as assessed by procurement teams who usually had no expertise in delivering domestic violence and abuse services), could bid for.

Critically, this moved the ownership of specialist women's services from the independent women/survivor-led organisations who had developed them, to the state. They were no longer *our* services. The specialist services that women's organisations had grown and developed over decades weren't ours anymore, they belonged to the local authority. The local authority became commissioners and were empowered to decide who delivered these services. And so, over time, the bidding wars started and slowly but surely, these little contracts were won by larger organisations, a good number of which are not women-led or woman-centred.

This was a big shift in power dynamics, and also came with a growing (and not unfounded) realisation that if the specialist organisations seemed to challenge local authorities, they had the power to give our funding to someone else. Community-based services, as well as accommodation-based ones, soon also followed this model.

One of the things that this process – competitive tendering – encouraged was lower cost bidding. When a contract goes out to tender, bids are assessed with a set percentage of points for quality and a set percentage for cost. The worst example I saw was a contract where bids were assessed with 70 percent of points on the basis of cost and 30 percent on quality. More often, mercifully, it is closer to the other way around. So, not only are smaller organisations who can't benefit from cost economies penalised, bidders are encouraged to bid low. If a local authority advertised a contract for a million pounds a year, bidders will not be thinking 'what can we do with a million pounds a year?' but 'what is the cheapest way that we can deliver what the contract requires of us?'

Over time local authorities began including the need to deliver services to men in their contracts, though more for community-based support services, like Independent Domestic Violence Advocates (IDVAs) rather than accommodation-based (refuge) services. Organisations which had been run by women for women had to decide whether or not to bid for contracts that included delivery to men or face the loss of important sources of income, without which they may have had to close down. Many local authorities began to include specialist services for women from Black and minoritised ethnic groups in one big contract, where there may previously have been a specialist 'by and for' group delivering those services. Southall Black Sisters (SBS) successfully challenged such a move in 2007/8. Ealing Council decided that the contract for domestic violence provision should be for a service that was accessible to all, irrespective of 'gender', sexual orientation, race, faith, age and disability, but SBS's services were for Black and Asian women only. This, therefore, would prevent them from bidding, unless they offered their service to everyone. SBS took Ealing Council to court – and won. The council conceded that specialist services provided by a specialist organisation was both lawful and necessary. Moreover, that such provision was anti-discriminatory and furthered objectives of equality and cohesion.[8] This was an important victory but many specialised groups providing services led and delivered by and for women from minoritised ethnic groups have not been so fortunate; this is the case for many other woman-led services.[9]

In short, ownership has been transferred from the independent women/survivor small organisations who developed and grew the services in the first place to local authorities. Local authorities, not women's groups, now define what is needed to be delivered and competitive tendering ensues. Large organisations with specialist bid-writers, or teams of bid-writers, have a big advantage over small specialist organisations, where staff have had to not only learn how to write bids, but fit this around the rest of their jobs. Lots of women-led organisations have since been forced to close down; in some cases these have merged with or been taken over by other larger women's organisations, but often not by women's organisations at all, such as Hesta, Sacro, Lookahead Housing.

nia, the organisation I work for, lost a refuge contract in 2011. The organisation that won the contract made the children's workers redundant when they took it over. They negotiated with each employee who had legal rights of employment under the new contract so that they had a longer working week and less annual leave in return for a one-off payment. New staff were appointed on lower salaries. They stopped taking in women who were dealing with more complex problems and they stopped offering 24-hour admissions to women needing emergency refuge accommodation. In 2021, I was copied into an email from the organisation about the number of refuge vacancies they had going into the weekend. The email also said that they would not accept anyone after 2.30pm on a Friday afternoon, so any woman who could not meet the deadline would need to be 'safeguarded over the weekend'. When nia had held the contract, if it was necessary for a woman's safety, we would have accepted the referral and found a way to admit her into the refuge at whatever time of day she could reach us. When vital services like refuges start to be seen as contracts, and not the lifelines for women and children that they are, it is the women and children who need them who lose out.

Most of the larger organisations now delivering services to women who have been subjected to men's violence lack the feminist politics of the organisations that have been subsumed. For many of us working in feminist-led organisations that are charities, campaigning and influencing the government to better address the needs of women, in particular those who have been subjected to men's violence, is integral to what we do and runs alongside the services that we provide. A cynical woman might observe that it suits those with patriarchal power to silence feminist organisations by surreptitiously removing our bite by taking away funding. When nia lost the refuge contract, it had such a detrimental effect on the stability of the charity that we were concerned that we would be forced to close down. Given that we were the first charity in the UK who supported women victims of men's violence to speak up for single-sex services,[10] the potential impact that the demise of our proudly feminist organisation might have had is evident. Would someone else have stood up? We can't know, of course, but it is possible that the loss of nia would have had grave consequences beyond the closure of the charity itself.

In fact, the government was aware of the potential power of charities to affect agendas. In 2016, although not specifically about women's rights, charities had worked together to resist an anti-advocacy clause (also known as the gagging clause) that the government had intended to include in all future grant agreements. This gagging clause would not permit charities to use such funds for 'activity intended to influence or attempt to influence Parliament, government or political parties, or attempting to influence the awarding or renewal of contracts and grants, or attempting to influence legislative or regulatory action'.[11] So perhaps the cynical woman might not be so wrong. And governments are using funding contracts to push their agendas. When the Scottish government set out conditions for its 2020–2023 funding stream, the 'Delivering Equally Safe Fund' (delayed until 2021–2024 due to the coronavirus pandemic), the guidance stated that all applicants 'must ensure that the service is inclusive to lesbian, bisexual, trans and intersex (LBTI) women'. At the same time, it did also state that organisations had the ability to utilise the single-sex exceptions in the Equality Act where that was a proportionate approach to achieving a legitimate aim. However, in 2021 North Lanarkshire council ceased funding Monklands Women's Aid, Motherwell District Women's Aid and North Lanarkshire Women's Aid, reportedly because they do not accept males into their refuges, or work with perpetrators, and instead awarded the funding to an offender rehabilitation organisation, Sacro.[12] Indeed, proud claims of going 'beyond the law' are regularly made by those advocating for transgender ideology, with little regard to the impact that this has on women. For example, the First Minister of Scotland, Nicola Sturgeon, has made clear that she backs 'gender recognition' reforms and dismissed as 'not valid' concerns raised by women seeking to protect women's rights.[13] Specialist providers of services for women in Scotland are being given mixed messages.

The problem extends beyond Scotland. In 2021, RISE, a charity that had supported women for over 26 years, lost its contract with Brighton and Hove City Council, East Sussex County Council and the Office of the Sussex Police and Crime Commissioner as a result of a retendering process. Nicola Benge, who had been supported by the charity for four years, told me:

> My concern as a service user has been that the charity was defunded largely as a result of not being sufficiently 'inclusive', despite already having an award-winning LGBT service that it has offered for a number of years as an adjunct to their existing

services. I am so cross about this trend, but more than this, I am afraid. Afraid for women like me who have no access to women-only services and safe single-sex spaces in my own city any longer. It is not fair, it is not right and we must fight this.

Vancouver Rape Relief & Women's Shelter is Canada's longest running rape crisis centre and has resisted pressures to become mixed-sex, including when the city council withdrew funding because the services were for females only. The decision to withdraw funding occurred after the organisation had resisted the actions of a transwoman, Kimberly Nixon, in 1995, who filed an ultimately unsuccessful complaint after being turned down for a place for volunteer counsellors.[14]

Those women-led organisations that have survived frequently have to bid for our services every three or so years – and are under no illusion where the power lies. The transfer of ownership created by the competitive tendering process happened before most organisations were aware of, or were dealing with, the issue of including males with a transgender identity in what were supposed to be women-only services. But the reason it's important to understand this transfer of power is because I believe it profoundly affected women's organisations' sense of their own vulnerability and confidence in standing up to or challenging their local authority, and this has affected their willingness to openly protect single-sex provision.

Supporting People wasn't all bad. It did push up standards in some areas because the grant came with an assessed quality framework, a sort of OFSTED for supported housing. But the way support was delivered widened the gap between staff and 'service users'. In fact, it made ubiquitous the phrase 'service user', and made the 'us and them' split unavoidable in the name of professionalisation. Those of us running and working in refuges had to make sure that what we did was deemed good practice in a national framework which had not been developed for – and did not specifically address the needs of – women fleeing abusive men.[15] And it was not remotely woman-centred or trauma-informed. This pushed the feminist understanding of men's violence against women and girls further out of sight. This doesn't mean that everyone delivering specialist services to women has abandoned feminism: nia hasn't and no one could accuse Southall Black Sisters or Latin American Women's Rights Service of skimping on feminist politics. The same remains true of several other women-led organisations.

The Supporting People programme doesn't exist any longer, but the transfer of ownership of contracts away from specialist services developed by women in response to women's needs has remained and become embedded. This was followed by the austerity drive from 2008 onwards following the global financial crisis. Local authority grants from central government were cut in many areas, which meant that some local authorities also chose to deliver services (especially those which are community-based rather than accommodation-based, like refuges) in-house, so they became council delivered rather than delivered by independent women's organisations. For some women, this means that they may be less likely to contact them when they need them because it is a common abuser tactic for men to tell women that their children will be taken away from them if they try to get help. Independent research[16] has identified this too, but too many local authorities choose to ignore that council-run services for women who have been subjected to men's violence are a barrier to access for many women.

Funding for organisations supporting women who have been subjected to sexual violence, including rape, was often, and arguably remains, the poor relation compared with domestic violence and abuse. The funding has substantially increased over the last ten years, in no small part due to the work of Rape Crisis England and Wales, working to both increase provision and ensure that only those with the appropriate skills deliver it. Most services are funded through contracts. In some areas, some of these are delivered by what I would consider inappropriate organisations; in others, it seems that commissioners actually understand the importance of specialist organisations with a track record of delivery. Though, as I will address later, this hasn't stopped some organisations deciding to end their single-sex provision.

Those developing the first refuges in the 1970s would be amazed to see the resources now directed to services for women who have been subjected to men's violence, but I think the separation from feminist politics would be equally shocking to them. What I want readers to understand from this chapter is how, in the space of 50 years, we started from a place of formidable feminist collective energy and action pulling together and creating new services to support women who had been subjected to men's violence. Within a couple of generations, we have come to a place where many, if not the majority, of those working in the same organisations and supporting later generations of victim-survivors of men's violence seem to have lost their political edge. What happened to the willingness or ability to stand up for women's sex-based rights and protections, to the understanding of the patriarchal context of men's violence against women?

4

What Difference Does it Make?

The need for women-only spaces for women who have been subjected to men's violence

In this chapter I am going to look at some of the reasons that women who are rebuilding their lives after men's violence and abuse need women-only spaces. I will examine the question of whether risk assessments can be used so that we could look at services on the basis of gender identification rather than sex, which would, of course, make them mixed-sex. After that, I'm going to look at trauma in women victim-survivors of men's violence and the differences that single-sex services can make. I'll address gaslighting, power dynamics and how important it is that women who are recovering from men's violence and abuse learn to trust and believe in themselves.

As I survey the needs of women who have been subjected to men's violence in this chapter, it is with the understanding that all services must provide equitable services to women who have been abused by men. And, because of structural inequality, this doesn't mean treating everyone the same; it means recognising that some must have different services because of particular inequalities. And, that Black, Asian and women from other minoritised communities should have access to specialised services delivered by women with whom they share a racial and/or cultural heritage, whether that is because such services better meet their needs or as a matter of choice. In 2020, there were only 18 specialist 'by and for' Black and minoritised women's refuges remaining in the whole of the UK.[1]

Meanwhile, if those who identify as transwomen pose a risk to women, it is not because they are trans, but because they are male. Male bodies are bigger and stronger, and thus they are more capable of causing harm if their owner so wishes. Most males have a penis. As I have discussed already, most males who say they have transitioned still have a penis, regardless of whether or not they have obtained a Gender Recognition Certificate. And males commit violence at much higher rates than females.

Risk assessment – women's refuges

It has been claimed by transgender activists and their allies that it is possible to use risk assessments of males so that any risk that they might pose to women using single-sex services is removed. For example, in the WESC Transgender Equality report, one extensively quoted witness, Peter Dunne, a Visiting Researcher, from New York University Law School, said:

> [A]ll of the research seems to be saying that if you are able to put in place robust frameworks that explain to people everyone's presence in the particular shelter and that everyone knows all of the ground rules and has a clear understanding, these facilities work perfectly well and inclusion in no way detracts from the ability of individuals to use the services and their experience.[2]

Presumably the assumption is that any potential risks posed will be identified and mitigated against, or that a person will not be permitted to access the services in question if risks

that cannot be removed or reduced are identified. This fun-
damentally misunderstands the purpose of risk assessments
in the delivery of services to women who have survived men's
violence and abuse. If we can remove something (males) and
in doing so remove the risk posed, we need a very good reason
for *not* doing so.

The women-only refuge movement was founded upon risk
assessment, though I'm pretty sure it wasn't called that then.
What was being assessed was the risk of men's violence. The
perpetrators of that violence were and are men. We've known
for some time that leaving an abusive man can heighten the
risk that he will use escalated levels of violence as he tries to
regain the control that he has lost. Jane Monckton Smith says
that when we are looking at risk of intimate partner femicide (the killing of a woman by her partner or ex-partner), the
process is motivated by control rather than a response to an
incident.[3] Coercive control, she says, is 'frequently driven by
the fears of its perpetrators, and maintained by the fears of its
victims'.[4] The Femicide Census looked at separation as a factor
in intimate partner femicide. We found that at least two out of
every five women who are killed by current or former partners
in the UK have separated or taken steps to separate from them.
Of these, at least a third are killed within a month of separation
and three-quarters within the first year.[5] The biggest risk to a
woman in a refuge is almost always her former partner.

When a woman, and often her children too, are moving into
a refuge, risk and needs assessments are completed with her
so that staff can be sure that the refuge will offer her a place of
safety and be able to meet her needs. The first part of the risk
assessment is completed over the telephone before a woman is
told how to get to the refuge and where it is. The main focus
of the assessment is the safety of the woman (and where applicable, her children), though a check on whether the woman
herself may be a risk to anyone living in the refuge is also
included. To address the first question, a simple check is made

of whether the location of the refuge is too close to where the man she is escaping from, usually her now ex-partner, lives, works or socialises to avoid the risk of her or the children crossing paths with him. Usually the children have to change schools so that they or their mum can't be found through the school. To address the second part, questions are asked about whether the woman has a history of violence or dangerous behaviour such as arson. The main aim, when a risk assessment is being completed with a woman moving into a refuge, is to get her to a place of safety as quickly as possible.

Risk assessments are not intended to address whether a male is a suitable person to live in a women's refuge. It is much more effective to keep them all away. Refuges are single-sex largely, but not only, in recognition of the fact that it is males who pose a threat to women's safety and one of the most effective means by which we can keep women and children in refuges safe is by keeping males out of them.

The function of a risk assessment is not to ascertain whether a male who claims to have transitioned and who may still retain fully intact and functioning male genitalia is a risk to the women and children in the refuge. Risk assessments used by women's refuges are certainly not intended to assess whether a male who claims to have transitioned has done so in a way that some would consider meaningful; regardless of whether or not he has had surgery and hormones, he retains the personality characteristics of someone who has been socialised as a male and possesses greater strength.[6] Risk assessments for women's refuges are not intended to assess whether a male is claiming to have transitioned as an attempt to try and locate a particular woman who may have left him and to whom he is a serious risk, or whether or not he is using the process to gain access to vulnerable women or to satisfy a narcissistic need for validation. A Gender Recognition Certificate, whether attained through self-identification or a verification process, does not change a person's actual sex; it does not undo years or decades of sex-role socialisation and it will not stop an abusive male from being abusive.

If you recommend telephone risk assessments as a means to keep women in refuges safe, you are expecting a member of staff, in the course of a telephone call, to differentiate between (1) a transgender person born male, who will not be a threat to women in the refuge and who has overcome the trappings of male socialisation, who is genuinely in fear of violence and (2) a male (with or without a transgender identity) who is steeped in the vestiges of male socialisation, (3) one who may be a predator exploiting a loophole, (4) one who resents women, or (5) one whose interest is his own validation and not the needs of the women in the refuge; or finally (6) just a man who is pretending to be transgender in an attempt to track down a particular woman or just to have access to vulnerable women.

I have over thirty years' experience of providing support to women who have been abused by men. No one has yet put forward a convincing case for how risk assessment is suddenly supposed to be used to assess which males are safe to be accommodated in refuges. Risk assessment is about identifying risks posed by violent men and mitigating against them, not adding risks because some people now say that males can be women.

I have seen that a small number of organisations who run refuges say that they are considering making the self-contained accommodation they have available to males with transgender identities, whilst keeping the communal spaces in more traditional refuges with more shared facilities women-only. Where it is available, self-contained refuge accommodation is often the most desirable and sought-after for obvious reasons. It isn't easy uprooting yourself and your children and finding yourself sharing a kitchen, bathroom and living room with other women and children; it can be stressful. In practice, this means that those organisations are making their most comfortable accommodation open to males while decreasing women's access. The 2021 Women's Aid annual survey found that, as always, demand was higher than the provision available, with 57.2 per cent of refuge referrals declined during the year – 18.1 per cent of all referrals were turned down due to lack of capacity in the refuge.[7] There is not enough refuge provision available to meet the needs of women who need it, and yet some groups are making their services, in some cases their most comfortable accommodation, open to males. I'm aware that this can come about as a result of pressure from commissioners, but I think feminist organisations focused on supporting women should do just that and resist this pressure. And if they are making a choice, then I think they have their priorities wrong. I was informed anecdotally that equalities impact assessments rarely indicate a need for extra refuge provision for transgender males, unless in the cities with a larger population of males who identify as transgender, but almost always indicate underprovision for women.

Risk assessments do not provide a gateway for males, regardless of any transitioning process, to safely be admitted to a woman-only refuge for women fleeing abusive men. Even if they did, the physical safety of women and the risk of men's violence is not the only reason that refuges best meet women's needs by being single sex, as I will address later in this chapter.

Risk assessments – community-based services

Other sorts of services for women who have been subjected to men's violence and abuse use different forms of risk assessments.

The first, like in most workplaces, is used to identify any potential hazards and what must be done to prevent them from happening and minimise the harmful impact that they may have if they do.

The second is the risk assessment model for women accessing community-based domestic violence and abuse services.
The risk-based model has been widely criticised but remains
in favour with government and commissioners. Because it
is local government bodies and commissioners who decide
what is delivered in local areas, a risk-based model of services
remains. It aims to identify those at greatest risk of serious
harm (including homicide) so that resources can be prioritised
to where need is greatest; in other words, the most support
goes to those most at risk. But there is a growing body of
research that says that the most common risk assessment procedures do not do this effectively.[8] Expert analyst of domestic
violence interventions Davina James-Hanman adds that the
focus of support has

> moved away from empowering survivors – and arguably even
> listening to them describe their needs and experiences – and
> become focused on risk, prosecution and information shar-
> ing. When the last Labour Government finally capitulated to
> demands for a national Violence Against Women strategy in
> 2009, it was notable how much of the content was criminal
> justice system-focused, even though this was utilised by a
> minority of survivors.[9]

This mirrors what I described in chapter 3 about the loss of
feminist politics from the delivery of refuges. Regardless, it
isn't the *type* of risk assessment used – in theory – to assess the
level of risk posed to a woman by her male current or former
partner that people are talking about when they're claiming
that risk assessments can be used to remove the problems
associated with allowing males to live in women's refuges.

Trauma – and trauma-informed environments

Trauma isn't a bad thing that happens to someone or a bad thing that happened in the past. It is the lasting effect that the bad thing or things has.

It's not unusual for women who've been subjected to men's violence to develop a trauma response. These sometimes develop after a single incident of extreme violence, particularly with regard to sexual violence, though sometimes it can develop after years or months of living in fear, walking on eggshells, recognising that tone of voice, that look in the eyes, that sigh, that pause, that silence, that change in his breathing. Some women have lived this all their lives, with a succession of perpetrators beginning with their dad – who may have been physically, sexually or emotionally violent, abusive and controlling or a mixture of them all. Research has shown that when we are trapped or pinned down in a situation where our urge to escape cannot be acted upon, for example if we are pinned down during sexual and/or domestic violence, the brain keeps releasing the stress hormones and this may continue after the threat has passed.[10] It seems that being in a situation where you are able to do something to protect yourself can have a strong influence on whether or not the experience will have a long-lasting impact.

Post-traumatic stress disorder (PTSD) can develop in response to trauma that may have occurred recently or in the distant past. Those who have experienced sexual trauma, especially whilst young, are at greater risk, with victims of multiple forms of childhood abuse and neglect most at risk of lifetime trauma.[11] Women victim-survivors of childhood sexual abuse are at least twice as likely to experience adult sexual victimisation.[12] According to a 2016 study, 51 per cent of adults who were abused as children experienced domestic abuse in later life and approximately one in six adults who were abused as a child had been subjected to domestic violence and abuse in the previous year.[13]

Studies of women involved in prostitution found that between 63 and 80 per cent reported being subjected to violence in the course of being prostituted.[14] One study found that women in prostitution were murdered at a rate twelve times above that of non-prostituted women.[15] Many women in prostitution describe sexual encounters as non-consensual, coerced or economically coerced rape. Two-thirds of women in prostitution suffer PTSD.[16]

PTSD/trauma responses happen in a part of the brain called the amygdala. The amygdala detects a threat or perceived threat and can activate a 'fight-or-flight' response. This happens to most of us in threatening situations. It releases adrenaline, norepinephrine and glucose into the body, and cortisol if the threat continues. A part of the prefrontal cortex (an area in the front of the brain that processes emotions and behavioural reactions) assesses the threat and can either calm us or reinforce the fight-or-flight response.

People suffering trauma/PTSD have a hyper-reactive amygdala and a less effective calming prefrontal cortex reaction. The stress hormones can spike more quickly and in response to what for others might only be mildly stressful or agitating and they take longer to return to baseline levels. In other words, after trauma, the brain can be triggered by something that would barely register for someone else, interpreting something that for many people would be unthreatening as a serious threat or danger, for example the presence of a man, particularly where not expected. Referring to PTSD survivors, psychiatrist Abram Kardiner explained that they could 'develop a chronic vigilance for and sensitivity to threat'.[17] In other words, they are frequently 'on edge'.

Trauma is pre-verbal. Bessel van der Kolk, a Dutch psychiatrist who lives and works in the US, and specialises in trauma and PTSD, likens the amygdala to the brain's smoke detector. Its job is to identify anything that is a threat to survival and, if it senses one, to send a message down the hypothalamus and the brain stem, firing up the stress hormones and making our body respond, sometimes before we've even consciously thought about it.[18]

Research on brain activity in people who experienced flash-backs or nightmares after traumatic experiences showed that when they were experiencing flashbacks, Broca's area, the part of the brain that deals with verbalisation, registered no activity. Instead, an area in the visual cortex, Brodmann's Area 19, registered activity. This means, rather than recalling past events, the brain's response during flashbacks was as if the trauma was actually occurring at the time.[19]

Becoming numb, shutting down and struggling to interact with the present can be the flipside of the PTSD/trauma coin. The brain becomes overwhelmed by the trauma (causing prefrontal cortex shutdown) leading to disorientation and confusion as the higher brain functions of reasoning and language are disrupted. Thinking and reasoning can be drowned out by feeling and being. Prolonged stress can lead to permanent change in the prefrontal cortex. Working with army veterans, van der Kolk observed that they often reported feeling dead inside, whereas the only time they felt alive was when they were in highly dangerous situations. Whether stressful experiences lead to a person shutting down or feeling more agitated, even 'alive', it becomes much harder to calmly and rationally control your impulses, emotions and reactions.

Recovery from trauma requires a visceral feeling of safety. Van der Kolk states, 'trauma almost invariably involves not being seen, not being mirrored, and not being taken into account'. So, when we're providing spaces or services for women who have been subjected to men's violence, it's important that we recognise that a significant number of them will be suffering from trauma. In other words, our space or service should be trauma-informed. Not everyone will need this but large enough numbers of women will for it to justify prioritising it in the design of our project or service. We shouldn't focus on the needs of people who don't need something that we provide when we can create something that works for every abused woman from the start. We should not ignore that women are socialised to put the needs of others before their own, and should understand the impact of socialisation. A trauma-informed safe space creates room for action and recovery from violence and abuse and places the woman victim-survivor in control and in the centre.

The trauma response described earlier is the antithesis of a foundation for action and recovery, so a trauma-informed approach must be based on understanding the physical, social and emotional impact of trauma caused by experiencing violence and abuse. A trauma-informed service for women understands the importance of creating an environment – physical and relational – that feels safe to victim-survivors in all the ways I've just mentioned. The presence of males, including those who may not identify as men but whom victim-survivors recognise as such, can trigger some women's trauma response. Their presence might mean that victim-survivors of men's violence cannot relax, that they constantly feel on edge, hyper-vigilant, nervous, ready for fight or flight. The exclusion of males from their recovery space, and yes, this includes those who don't identify as men, can support the recovery of many women. Individual men's behaviour and the likelihood that any biological male may or may not be abusive is not relevant in this situation. Women experiencing trauma after violence and abuse will, like most of us, almost always instantly read someone – who might be the most kind and gentle trans-identifying male in the world – as male, and they may experience a debilitating trauma response as a result. It's not their fault, it's not a choice and it's not something they can be 'educated out of'. It's not hate. It's not bigotry. It's not transphobia. It is an impact of abuse by men. In order to recover and heal, women need space, support and sometimes therapy – not increased confrontation with a trauma-inducing trigger; and not a mixed-sex space. The resistance to males in abused women's spaces is not about the individual trans person, it is about the women who need to recover.

Rachel Hewitt, a writer and academic, wrote an account of being raped on her birthday during the first year of her doctorate at the University of Oxford. She said

I had never before felt my body, so directly, to be the recipient of male violence; a battlefield for a struggle between autonomy and patriarchal oppression. And I had never before felt so directly betrayed by male authority figures charged with my care, and male friends. I had also never before felt the worth of, the visceral need for, female company: for women whose bodies had, like mine, made them vulnerable to particular types of male encroachment, confinement and intimidation, from the moment of birth onwards. A female therapist, female friends, feminism: these things made all the difference.[20]

To properly heal from trauma, in particular that caused by sexual violence, a course of counselling/therapy from a counsellor/therapist specially trained to deal with trauma/PTSD from sexual or domestic violence and abuse may be needed. Unfortunately, far too few women are offered this opportunity. Specialist women-led, women-only organisations supporting victim-survivors of men's violence are rarely funded to the extent that we can meet the levels of need that exist. As I discussed in chapter 3, too often we're contracted to do what commissioners value, but this isn't always what women want and need.

Not all women will be subjected to men's violence and abuse, though globally one in three are at some point during their lifetime. Not all women who are subjected to men's violence and abuse will develop a trauma response. Not all women who have been abused by men want women-only spaces – but should this then deny the right of that space for those who do?

Women who have been subjected to men's violence and who are living with PTSD or a trauma response deserve somewhere to feel safe and relax. They deserve head space, somewhere where they don't feel on-guard all the time, consciously or not, because of the presence of men. Women-only space for women who have been subjected to men's violence and abuse is something that must be protected by those of us who don't need it and, for those of us who do.

Gaslighting – re-learning to trust our own judgement

Gaslighting is a common tactic used by abusers to manipulate their victim(s), making them doubt their own judgement and question their perception. It is a form of emotional abuse which is used to break down self-confidence and increase dependence on the abuser, another way to create coercive control. The term comes from a play called 'Gaslight', released in 1938 and set in the Victorian era, which was released as a film in the 1940s. Bella Manningham is married to an abusive man who it later turns out murdered her aunt. Every twilight, he 'disappears' to the sealed off floors above their apartment where the wealthy aunt's belongings are stored. Guided by shadowy gaslights, his searches upstairs for the aunt's jewels inadvertently cause the lights in the rest of the apartment to dim. He tries to convince Bella that she is going insane, and that she is imagining the dimming of the lights, the footsteps that she can hear from the floor above, that she is moving objects and forgetting that she moved them. As a form of abuse, gaslighting can involve denying that something was said or insisting that someone did or said things that they didn't, undermining the other person's version of events, convincing them that they're too sensitive, in short, undermining their grasp on reality.

I consider the pressure to repeat and internalise the mantra 'transwomen are women', repeated by many trans rights activists and lobbyists, to be large-scale gaslighting, something that has been used as propaganda to coerce individuals and institutions into compliance. It is not enough to say that one supports universal human rights, and opposes violence against or harassment of people who identify as having a gender identity in opposition to the stereotypes associated with their sex, or to say that one celebrates those who confound the shackles of gender. People cannot and do not actually change sex, and I believe the word 'woman' should be defined in relation to sex. Furthermore, I believe that most people know that people cannot actually change sex, even when they say the opposite.

The tactic has been so successful that demonstrating one's allegiance to the orthodoxy leads intelligent people to walk willingly into logical and linguistic dead ends. When explaining on BBC Politics that she believed the majority of people held the view that 'transwomen are women', the journalist and commentator Ellie Mae O'Hagan, was asked about the definition of 'woman as biological sex'. She replied 'You know, I actually don't know why some people are women and why some people are men. No one on this panel does, and anyone who claims to know the answer to that question is a liar.' I suspect that this isn't true of most people. Unless someone doesn't understand reproduction or evolution, then they do know why some people are considered women and others are men, but demonstrating adherence to the prevailing orthodoxy can be more compelling than declaring the truth. Indeed, I can categorically say that I am not lying when I say that I know the difference between women and men – and can quite easily explain it.

Van der Kolk writes 'Learning to trust is a major challenge.' He continues, 'in order to know who we are . . . we must know (or at least feel that we know) what is and what was "real". We must observe what we see around us and label it correctly.'[21]

Why is this important when we're talking about women's refuges?

When you've been told that you're stupid or mad for long enough, being told something that is clearly false by someone who tells you that they are on your side can be extremely confusing. Working with a woman who has been abused by her partner often involves supporting her in re-learning to trust her own judgement and her ability to make decisions. It can involve helping her to identify and trust her own feelings, to give herself permission to be upset, angry or afraid when she was previously told that such responses were disproportionate or irrational. Honesty and respect are a critical part of this process, building self-trust and trust in others.

Staff working in refuges and hostels, whether they like it or not, whether they see all people as being equal or not, hold power and authority by virtue of the position they hold. They may manage that power respectfully and with integrity but it is always there. The women living in the refuge know that staff have the ability to take away their licence to occupy the refuge, to have them removed if they break the rules. Sometimes they have seen it happen to someone else, most likely someone who was sometimes difficult to live with, but nevertheless they felt bad after she was told she had to leave. If staff in refuges insist that something is true when it is clear to the eyes of a woman who has been abused that it is not true, she is left with the choice of doubting herself or doubting the person or people that she is learning to trust. When your self-belief is fragile or non-existent, this can be uncomfortable, even overwhelming.

Service providers are in a position of power, no matter how hard they try to balance this out, and of course the good ones do as much as possible to do so, but ultimately it is inescapable. Those working in and running a refuge or therapeutic group work space are not offering the trauma-informed environment that I discussed earlier in the chapter if they, in their position of power, gaslight traumatised women and insist that someone that they both know to be biologically male, should be referred to and treated as a woman.

It is furthering abuse to then expect women to share space – space which staff and service providers describe as women-only space – with males who say that they are women. This is because many of these women who have little choice but to be there understand viscerally that these 'males' are not women. Part of the role of those supporting women who are rebuilding their lives after men's violence and all the knock-on impacts of abuse is to help women to learn to trust themselves again – not to replace the lies with which their abuser has filled their head with a new version. Not to replace the doubt in their heads about their perception with a false reality, and not to make them feel bad about themselves by accusing them of bigotry.

Imagine moving into a women's refuge after having been told that your teenage son cannot come with you and so being forced to make the awful decision about whether to leave him living with his abusive father or finding somewhere else for him to go only to arrive and see that there is an adult male living there. You might have been told that your son could not live with you out of respect for the safety, privacy and well-being of other women in the refuge, but then be expected to believe that these concerns do not apply to a man with a transgender identity. If you had been feeling guilty about not being able to bring your son with you but recognised that you might have to go into a refuge to protect your life – or the lives of your children – how much worse might that make you feel?

Women's refuges are unique spaces. Before we had the language of risk assessment, trauma-informed environments and gaslighting, feminists, activists and survivors (who are not mutually exclusive) understood the importance of single-sex, women-only spaces. Women-only refuges for women who have been subjected to men's violence offer safety: physical and psychological safety, space to decompress and rebuild and to peel away self-blame and shame though sharing spaces with other women who have been there. Women-only centres for sexual violence survivors, including prostitution survivors and women-only therapeutic groups are also critical spaces for recovery and for moving on.[22] Nevertheless, some of those running the refuge apparently deem it appropriate to provide a trans-inclusive service.[23,24] The objection to adult men in women's therapeutic spaces and refuges is not about transgender males, whatever their background and presentation. Not all transgender people who are biologically male are violent, sexual abusers or autogynophiles (becoming sexually aroused at the thought of themselves as a woman).[25] Just as not all men are violent or abusive towards women and the majority are loving partners, fathers and friends. Nonetheless, our society has recognised through evidence, legislation, social convention and safeguarding procedures, that the percentage of men who do abuse women and girls is enough of a threat to justify single-sex spaces. There is no reason to suppose that the same considerations should not be applied to males who identify as trans.

I don't claim that refuges or other services can provide the framework for fully recovering from trauma for all women, since some women may need specialist therapeutic support for that, but they create the space for recovery for many women and children. Feeling safe is crucial. The logical part of the brain cannot undo the harm of trauma, and it cannot shut out feelings and emotions without safety. We, feminists who understand the impact of men's violence against women, should be defending the legacy of those who created successful and much-needed women's refuges for today's women and children – and until men stop abusing women and children – for those of the future.

Not all those who claim to support women, girls and children who have been subjected to men's violence with specialist services recognise the importance of single-sex spaces. There are a number of reasons for this. For those who accept that 'transwomen are women', this is a matter of trans rights and they insist that there should be no circumstances in which those who are biologically male but identify as women should be treated differently from women. Then there are those who believe that it is appropriate to act as if this were the case but, frankly speaking, have not thought through the implications. Then there are those who believe that transwomen should not be treated indiscriminately as women and that doing so has implications for females, but for whatever reason, have decided to stay quiet. We know from the treatment meted out to Allison Bailey,[26] Maya Forstater,[27] Raquel Rosario Sánchez,[28] Sonia Appleby,[29] Kathleen Stock,[30] Suzanne Moore[31] and Julie Bindel,[32] to name just a few, that there can be serious consequences for those who don't.

It is also important to recognise that refuges and some other services for women, for example hostels for homeless women, are usually services predominantly used by working-class women and women with limited options. Women with more resources do not usually have to resort to a refuge or a hostel to escape an abusive man. Women who are on state benefits are over-represented in women's refuges. Women with insecure immigration status have least choice of all. So those who seek to remove the sanctity of single-sex spaces because they themselves do not or have never needed them are denying them to the women who have fewest alternative options. In my view, this represents another example of identity politics failing to recognise the powerful dynamics of privilege and disadvantage.

A woman who uses the name Leonora Christina to protect her identity and who spent time living in a women's refuge to escape a violent man recalled a conversation with a woman who worked in a refuge. This woman believed that because no women had ever objected, there was no problem with the refuge employing a male. Leonora explained:

Women who enter refuge have no idea whether they are coming or going. They are traumatised, petrified and just need to be safe. They are not going to rock the boat when they first arrive. They don't want to be told to leave, that this isn't the place for them. They will do almost anything to keep safe, away from their abuser. If that means being retraumatised by the presence of a male no matter how he identifies, then they will. Especially when they have children. They're used to being told they have no agency, no right to decide who's in their space. Even the space staff will tell them it is women only. So they will keep quiet, just like they always do. Whilst being told that they are allowed to say 'no', they'll think that it doesn't apply in this instance. How could it be ok when the people in charge must think having a male in a woman's space is just fine? No one had given consent, no one had been aware that there was a male worker there before they arrived, these women had again been given no voice or choice. So, when I see posts about transgender inclusion, I know that the women in that refuge have not been given a choice. They have not been given a voice. They have not been made the absolute priority as they would have been promised they would be.

Asking women what they want

If we ask women victim-survivors of men's violence what they want, they consistently tell us that they want to be supported by women. The Equality and Human Rights Commission showed that 95 per cent of women using women's services preferred to receive them from a women-only organisation, and the preference for women-only services extended to healthcare, housing, substance use and probation services.[33] Another report found 79 per cent of women said that there was still a need for independent women's organisations even if mixed organisations and statutory bodies also provide single-sex services and that

99 per cent of the respondents believe that it is important for a woman who has been sexually assaulted or has experienced any other form of violence to have the choice to access a women-only support service. The reasons women gave for their preferences included safety, empathy, trust, comfort, support, less intimidating, focus on women's needs, shared identity, expertise, confidence, access, rapport and long-term care.[34] A study by the University of Suffolk found that survivors of childhood sexual abuse felt most believed by Independent Sexual Violence Advocates and rated the services provided by independent specialist organisations – women-run organisations – highest.[35] Aurora New Dawn asked over 600 women who had used their services what they thought: 100 per cent of those attending group work support wanted them to remain for women only and to be run by women only, and overall 93 per cent of all victim-survivors have a preference for a female member of staff.[36] Seventy-five per cent of lesbian survivors of same-sex partner abuse also stated a preference for support from women.[37]

Sex Matters is a UK-based, not-for-profit organisation campaigning to re-establish that sex matters in rules, laws, policies, language and culture. In 2022, they conducted an online survey about whether respondents thought single-sex services mattered and why. Of 7,000 respondents, 90 per cent were women, with 97 per cent of them stating there were circumstances in which single-sex provision mattered. The survey covered people's perspectives on hospital wards, intimate care, health services, toilets, face-to-face and online support groups and counselling for women experiencing menopause, breastfeeding and victim-survivors of sexual and domestic violence and abuse, Rape Crisis and refuge services, lesbian-only spaces and policing (after sexual assault). The most common reasons given for valuing single-sex services were privacy and dignity. The resulting report is a valuable repository of mainly women sharing their experiences and perspectives. However, reading it also made me feel sad and angry that women, yet again, must justify why women-only spaces are important. Women have had to make these arguments for centuries. It was clear in the report, as I posit throughout this book, that women did not want males with transgender identities excluded from women-only spaces because they were transgender, but because they were male.

Many women recounted abuse and episodes of voyeurism in mixed-sex facilities. Almost half of women respondents said they had experienced sexual assault. Women's comments included:

> Why trust all men? – the ones who assaulted me weren't trustworthy. How do you tell who is not going to do so? They do not have a mark on their forehead. Trust has to be earned.

> As a survivor, I often struggle with knowing when I am entitled to have boundaries. I really need the law to be on my side in this matter.

> When I have had to use gender-neutral facilities, I feel more on guard, I scan the surroundings more and check for access, exit and points of visibility. I feel more inhibited.

> A male nurse cared for my mother in hospital when she was close to death and it made her uncomfortable. She didn't have the strength to ask for a female nurse.[38]

Sarah's story

I am going to end this chapter with the story of Sarah Summers. This is Sarah's story, in her own words, about how she was let down by a rape crisis service which was supposed to support women victims of men's sexual violence and abuse.

> Like many women, I am a survivor of sexual violence. As a child I was tricked by a man I trusted into performing sex acts on

him. I was innocent and naïve; at the time I didn't even know what sex was, let alone sexual abuse. It was only when I reached adulthood that I realised he'd taken advantage of me.

My late teens involved toxic relationships with dubious men. I was a people pleaser with no idea how to set boundaries or say no.

In my 20s I made the bad decision of taking drugs with my 'friend' Joe. I had too much and lost consciousness. I woke up naked the following day with patchy recollections of Joe having sex with me while hitting me in the face. Since that night, seeing Joe or even hearing his name triggers a panic attack. It took me years to admit to myself that I hadn't consented to Joe's assault, that what he'd done to me was rape.

Having been badly let down by men in my life, I am wary of them. I know men can lie and manipulate, particularly if they have a sexual agenda. I live with chronic anxiety due to my negative experiences. I get stress-related migraines and suffer with digestive issues. I get nightmares and flashbacks.

I plucked up the courage to approach my local rape crisis centre for support and it was suggested I attend a female-only support group. I was apprehensive before attending the group but as soon as I met the other women my fears were alleviated. Finally, I'd met people who understood me. I attended the group every week and developed a strong bond with the other women. The space was kind and supportive, we had all been through similar experiences and it was a safe space to share our thoughts. We often talked about male entitlement and how much we appreciated having a space free from men where we could speak freely. I found the group helpful for my mental health and began to feel stronger.

After a couple of months, I arrived at the group as usual and was surprised to see someone who appeared to be a man. The facilitator started the session by saying pointedly 'everyone is welcome here'. I noticed the male attendee smiling as she said this. The mood of the group felt awkward and nobody volunteered to speak. The facilitator asked me directly how I had been feeling. I felt pressured to talk about my sexual violence so that the male service-user felt comfortable and included.

Feeling manipulated into prioritising the feelings of a male over my own instincts and boundaries felt familiar to me, it's something I have done since being sexually abused as a child. I masked my discomfort and spoke about my sexual violence to please the male person and provide the validation I knew was expected of me.

All the feelings that had been brought up from speaking about my sexual violence were there, but I had no outlet. There was nowhere I could turn to for help. Survivors like me believe transwomen to be men, and that makes them the embodiment of our abusers. I don't think requesting a rape crisis group where I wasn't reminded of my abuse was too much to ask.

Sarah Summers is pursuing legal action against Survivors Network.[39]

5

Looking Beyond

Services for women who have been subjected to men's violence aren't the only ones under threat

The issue of women-only space goes beyond supporting women who have been subjected to men's violence. Hospital wards, changing rooms (in shops and leisure spaces), toilets, projects to address the under-representation of women, political and social gatherings, prisons, women's prizes, marches, sport and festivals – all of these have increasingly become inclusive of males identifying as women. It is my belief that this, from some, including women, constitutes a refusal to acknowledge the right of women to define boundaries in ways which differ from their own. In others, again including some women, it may be an inability or unwillingness to empathise with some who need something that they do not, perhaps internalised misogyny, perhaps patriarchal female conditioning to 'be nice' or put men's needs first.

Women's safety, privacy, dignity, fairness, feminist organising or celebration are important considerations, but they are not the only ones. This chapter looks beyond single-sex services for women who've survived men's violence and abuse, and how the issue has fundamental ramifications for women's rights. I will look at a range of different spaces which are reserved for women, ranging from those created by women to those which have traditionally been single sex.

Women-only spaces created by women are not the reverse of men-only spaces and exclusionary boys' clubs. Women create those spaces as a response to sexism, a space away from male supremacy, rather than as an imitation of men and male culture. They are not spaces which allow us to wallow in and enjoy the benefits of being the dominant sex class. Neither are they a case of 'misandry' or reverse sexism. Although some male politicians objected to the Labour Party's women-only shortlists (for example, Peter Jepson and Roger Dyas-Elliott who were rejected as candidates), they work. Before all-women shortlists, the Labour Party had 37 female MPs, out of a total of 271 (13 percent).[1] After the 2019 election, 104 of Labour's 202 MPs were female.[2] Currently, the Party is not planning to use all-women shortlists in the next election, after legal advice warning that the system would be 'unlawful' because the majority of its MPs at that point were female.[3]

Women need the space to heal, share, acknowledge and celebrate. Being in a women-only space simply feels different. They offer an opportunity to appreciate diversity between women, how we differ and what we share. This also highlights that there are times when some women want, need or benefit from gathering within groups that are open to people with similar characteristics (e.g., class, race, culture, religion, disability, sexuality, motherhood or being childfree or childless).

Women-only prizes or shortlists exist in response to patriarchal structures which overlook women and present more barriers to participation. This is not the same as a golf club excluding women, or a university or profession excluding women because of obviously sexist assumptions about what women as a sex are capable of or are unsuited to.

Women's spaces are not only physical spaces, but also include women's bodies and shared experiences that are unique to womanhood and indeed girlhood. The feminist consciousness-raising groups that I mentioned in chapter 3 understood this and evolved as places for women to share the experiences that shaped and influenced us, understanding that whatever differences we faced, we all shared the experience of being female. I think those who use social media to troll women's #sharedgirlhood posts or promote transgender male experiences under that hashtag understand that too and are trying to breach the boundaries of women's experiential as well as physical spaces.

Meanwhile, feminism has not achieved its aims. There is still much for women to do, and we also know that when males are in mixed-sex space, they can easily dominate. When women are organising, especially to address the issue of sex inequality, we need to make sure it is our needs and our ideas that lead the solutions.

Prisons

Women make up approximately 4–5.5 percent of the prison population in the UK. Eighty per cent of women in prison are serving a sentence for a non-violent offence. Thirty-eight per cent of women in prison had been indicted for shoplifting (compared with 17 per cent of males)[4] and women are ten times more likely than men to be imprisoned for TV licence evasion, with a Ministry of Justice (MoJ) report admitting that the main reason for this is that women are more likely to open the door to inspectors.[5] The MoJ's Female Offender Strategy recognises that women offenders often 'pose a low or medium risk of serious harm to the public'.[6] Women from Black and other minoritised ethnic groups are over-represented, accounting for 11.9 per cent of the women's population in England and Wales, but 18 per cent of the women's prison population,[7] which reflects intersections of incarceration and poverty, racist policing and a racist criminal justice system, rather than disproportionate levels of criminality.

Together the GRA of 2004 and Equality Act of 2010 created the legislative pathway for males with transgender identities to enter women's prisons. In 2011, policy guidance stated that in most cases, prisoners must be located according to their gender as recognised by UK law.[8] Three cases which attracted significant media attention in 2015 raised the profile of the issue.[9] Tara Hudson, jailed for headbutting a bar manager after being refused alcohol, who had eight previous offences including for battery, and who did not hold a Gender Recognition Certificate, was transferred to a women's prison.[10] In November the same year, 21-year-old Vikki Thompson, who had been imprisoned for armed robbery, was found dead in HMP Leeds (a male prison). An inquest subsequently found that death by suicide was not intentional and that it had been correct for Vikki to be in the male estate.[11] A second transwoman, Joanne Latham, was found dead in a male prison in December. Latham was serving several life sentences, initially for attempting to murder a female friend and was subsequently found guilty of two other attempted murders whilst in prison. Latham had identified as a woman for four months and an investigation found that Latham was cared for appropriately in male facilities.[12]

Thereafter, the number of transgender people serving prison sentences rose from 70 in 2016, when the data was first collected, to 139 in 2018, then 163 in 2019, and finally to 197 in 2020[13] (the last year for which data are currently available). This represents a 181 per cent increase in five years. One hundred and fifty-eight (80 per cent) were males who identified as women, while 20 per cent identified as male. A further 10 males held Gender Recognition Certificates and in these cases the prisons recognised their gender identity instead of their sex, whether or not they had had any surgical interventions. In other words, they weren't included in the figures for transgender prisoners. The Ministry of Justice, who released the report, said that the numbers were unlikely to be accurate. According to the campaign group Keep Prisons Single Sex, 94 per cent of all male prisoners who identify as transgender are held in male prisons, whilst almost all those who have a GRC certificate are held in women's prisons.[14]

The WESC 2016 Transgender Equality report endorsed the 2011 policy guidance and argued that there was a 'clear risk or harm' where trans prisoners are not located in a prison 'appropriate to their acquired gender'.[15] The report appears to have less regard for the risk of harm to women posed by those claiming to be transgender as identified by the British Psychological Society in their written response to the inquiry, which warned of 'a number of cases where men convicted of sex crimes have falsely claimed to be transgender females . . . seeking better access to females and young children through presenting in an apparently female way'.[16]

Of a reported 4,890 transgender prisoners in the US, over 99 per cent are incarcerated according to their sex, with data from 45 states showing that 13 males were held in women's prisons and two females were held in men's prisons.[17] A survey of 29 transgender prisoners by the Prison Policy Initiative found that 23 (79 per cent) had been on probation before and over a third (11/29) had served time in jail at least twice before.[18] However, the small sample size represents less than 1 per cent of the transgender prison population and the study cannot be assumed to be representative. In recent years, however, states including Connecticut, Massachusetts and California have introduced processes of considering incarceration based on gender identity.[19] As in the UK, the safety and dignity of female prisoners appears to be an afterthought, as illustrated by a case filed by women prisoners in California, including Krystal Gonzalez, Tomiekia Johnson, Janine Chandler and Nadia Romero, which has alleged sexual assault by male transgender prisoners as well as a violation of their rights to safety, dignity, privacy and to practise their religion.[20]

In 2021, criminologist Jo Phoenix estimated that around 20 males with transgender identities, who may or may not have had surgery, were incarcerated in the UK's 12 women's prisons. In a speech delivered at a Woman's Place UK (WPUK) meeting in 2021, she said that of 129 transgender males in prison, 57 per cent had at least one conviction for sexual offences. This is compared with 18 per cent of the general male prison population and 2 per cent of the population of women in prison. According to this, males in prison with a transgender identity who do not hold a GRC are three times more likely than other males (i.e., those who do not identify as transgender) to have committed at least one sexual offence. No one is able to say whether males in prison with transgender identities are more likely to be sexual offenders or whether sexual offenders are more likely to adopt transgender identities. Moreover, whether or not we ourselves believe a person can be transgender, we do not know whether those males who claim this identity believe this themselves or whether it is a dishonest attempt to gain access to females or exert control in the prison environment. Regardless, these numbers tell us that males in prisons who identify as transgender pose a risk to women. Women who are incarcerated do not have the choice to remove themselves from the proximity of males who are a risk to them.

Addressing the WPUK meeting, Phoenix stated that the prison policy on including males who hold a GRC was not based on research or evidence: 'there have been no rigorous research projects that have analysed the policy from the point of view of the prisons as an organisation, from the prison staff, from the women in prison, or from the governors: none, it doesn't exist'. She continues that no research has asked the question of whether 'the panel who decide to transfer transgender prisoners take into account the women's thoughts and feelings'. Instead, she continued, given what we have learned about the undue influence of Stonewall, we might ask how much prison policy was shaped by one highly controversial model of transgender rights pushed by Stonewall and deemed to not affect women's rights, or if it did, deemed necessary despite any impact on women's rights.[21]

Most women in prison have suffered violence and abuse perpetrated against them (for which no one was ever convicted or incarcerated), which was worse than the crime for which they themselves were incarcerated. At least 70 per cent of women in prison are victim-survivors of domestic violence and abuse,[22] 53 per cent of women reporting having experienced emotional, physical or sexual abuse as a child.[23] For many women, incarceration and the withdrawal of their liberty may be the one time in their life that they are removed from men's violence and abuse. These are good reasons for us to expect that the prison environment should be trauma-informed. At the very least, that environment should be women only. We should be able to guarantee safety to women in prison. And yet we cannot.

Cheryle Kempton was assaulted by Karen White, previously Stephen Wood, at Newhall Prison in West Yorkshire.[24] Kempton has waived the lifetime anonymity granted by law to sexual assault victims to highlight the danger posed to women in prison by transgender inmates. White, who was over six foot, was granted privileges, such as access to make-up and wigs, which were not extended to women in the prison. White had stopped taking the hormones that not only stimulate breast growth but also reduce the ability to get an erection, concealing this from staff by hiding the tablets under the tongue. Cheryle Kempton was one of four women who have come forward to reveal that they were assaulted by White, who had previous convictions for sexually assaulting minors, grievous bodily harm and multiple rapes. White should never have been placed in a women's prison and no risk assessment or other paperwork would have made it safe for this to happen.

Kayleigh Woods did not hold a GRC when transferred to a women's prison in 2017. Woods was serving a life sentence for the murder of 20-year-old Bethany Hill. The 'transgender case

board'[25] had considered that a lack of sex offences on record
meant that Woods posed little risk to female prisoners. Yet,
Kayleigh Woods and a male lover had bound Bethany Hill
with duct tape before slashing her throat, inflicting multiple
wounds and leaving her to bleed to death. Far from there being
an absence of sexual motive, the judge who sentenced Woods
had outlined this very possibility for the murder. Woods was
moved back to a male prison after having sex with a female
inmate within weeks of entering the women's prison.[26]

Between 2016 and 2019, there had been seven officially
recorded sexual assaults where prisoners who identify as
transgender were involved out of a total of 97 reported sexual
assaults.[27] The real figures are likely to be higher as prison
culture discourages reporting, or 'grassing', to authorities.
Transgender inmates were five times more likely to carry out
sexual attacks compared with other prisoners with a documented history of assault.[28] Assaults by transgender inmates
had been recorded in New Hall, Low Newton, Co Durham,
Foston Hall in Derbyshire, and Bronzefield in Middlesex
and Peterborough. These reported attacks do not, of course,
include the intimidation of women and the impact on their
general well-being.[29] There are approximately 3,220 prisoners
in the female estate.[30] Jo Phoenix, whom I introduced earlier,
estimated that approximately 20 were males with transgender
identity (approximately 0.6 per cent) so approximately 3,200
are female. If we assume these figures were roughly constant
between 2016 and 2019, 0.6 per cent of the population committed 7 per cent of the sexual assaults; or there was roughly
one sexual assault for every three male transgender prisoners
in women's prisons compared with one sexual assault for every
36 women. Even allowing for some variation in the figures, it is
clear that women in prison are at much greater risk from male
transgender prisoners than they are from other women.

Women's rights to safety and dignity, whether they are
serving time in prisons or working in them, had clearly been

accorded secondary importance to the feelings, wishes and management issues posed by violent males in each of these cases. In his contribution to *Trans Britain*, James Morton, who until October 2020 was the manager of Scottish Trans Alliance, wrote that there had been a deliberate choice by trans rights activists to target prison policy so the principle of self-identification could be embedded there and then used as a precedent elsewhere to 'ensure that all other public services should be able to do likewise'.[31] According to Morton, using prison as an example would make it much easier to 'assist' other public services, including schools and the NHS, to respect people's gender identities. Former Scottish prison governor Rhona Hotchkiss has frequently lamented the impact of this policy on the well-being of women in prison in Scotland. In a 2020 interview with the BBC, she said, 'My experience is that it is always an issue to have transwomen in with female prisoners. I think you have to think beyond the obvious things like physical or sexual threat, which are sometimes an issue, to the very fact of the presence of a male-bodied person among vulnerable women causes distress and consternation.'[32]

The examples above alone make clear that risk assessments conducted by people with specialist knowledge and experience of working with offenders have repeatedly failed to keep women safe from dangerous males. Yet, as I discussed in chapter 4, the claim is made that those of us with experience of supporting women who have been abused by men (not violent offenders), should be using risk assessments to keep women safe from transgender males. If we know something isn't infallible when used by expert offender managers, why would we suddenly expect the same tool to work for those without that expertise? You could be forgiven for thinking that concern about women's safety has been chucked out of the window.

A 2021 High Court ruling (*FDJ v. SSJ*) deemed that it was lawful for transwomen to be housed in female jails, regardless of surgery, other medical interventions or whether they held a GRC certificate. Lord Justice Holroyde accepted that the statistical evidence showed higher levels of sexual offending in transgender males than in either other males or females in prison but said these should not be used for general conclusion. He also recognised that women might suffer fear and acute anxiety if sharing prison accommodation with males who have transgender identities.[33] It may be lawful, but that doesn't make it right.

Women's safe accommodation

Women's hostels, unlike refuges, support women who have become homeless for any reason. I worked in women's hostels for several years earlier in my working life. Almost always, women's homelessness is linked to men's violence and abuse.[34,35] It was often the case that women living in the hostels where I worked had not been accepted after being referred to refuges, usually because of problematic substance use or behaviour that was deemed difficult or disruptive. Either way, this itself was most often the result of abuse and trauma, particularly childhood sexual abuse, and research has long linked women's problematic substance use and childhood abuse.[36] Women living in women's hostels need every consideration of trauma afforded to women living in refuges. Already, however, males with transgender identities are being moved into women's hostels. In Fife, Scotland, transgender Katie Dolatowski was placed in a women's hostel after avoiding a prison sentence after sexually assaulting a 10-year-old girl, pushing her into a toilet and ordering her to take her trousers off, and, on a separate occasion, filming a 12-year-old over a toilet cubicle in a supermarket. The girl saw a mobile phone being held over the partition as she was sitting on the toilet. In court, Dolatowski, who was 18 at the time of the offences, admitted voyeurism and sexual assault charges. In other words, Katie Dolatowski had been shown to be a risk in supposed women-only spaces. Women's safety was risked and their well-being overlooked by placing Dolatowski in the hostel. Within months Dolatowski was back in court for breaching the terms of a community service order which had banned contact with children and also prohibited deletion of online search histories. At Kirkcaldy Sheriff Court, Sheriff Williamson said internet searches which Dolatowski had conducted were detailed in a report by social workers. He did not to read them out, but said they were 'alarming to say the least'.[37]

Mark Addis served six months on remand after threatening to kill his former partner before being handed an 18-month supervision order, 40 days on a domestic abuse perpetrator programme, and given an indefinite restraining order requiring him to stay away from his former partner. Despite his history of violence against women, an LGBTQ project referred Addis to an East London accommodation project where transgender males had access to the facilities in a women-only hostel. A member of staff who has since left the project said 'When the transwomen clients came into the women's hostel and started acting aggressively, the women were absolutely terrified.' They continued, 'The mantra was that transwomen are women and they are vulnerable. Even if they have a criminal record, if they are transitioning, they are not a risk anymore because they are women now. There was no room for debate. To even suggest you had an issue with that, that's it – you were out. It was really unsettling and terrifying for the women living at the hostel. These are women who are traumatised.'[38]

In Canada, a woman called Kristi Hanna was placed in a shared room in a hostel for women with problematic substance use with a trans-identifying male who had had no surgical interventions. She contacted the Human Rights Legal Support Centre but was told that she was being discriminatory because she described her roommate as a man. Kristi had been living in the facility for several months and was addressing her substance use problems and recovering from sexual abuse. After attempting to share the room with the new resident for two nights, she began to stay on friends' couches. In an interview, she said 'It's affecting everyone in the house. This can completely ruin your recovery, let alone your safety, let alone your life. We were all choked by our own anxiety, our crippling PTSD symptoms. You could cut the tension in the house.'[39]

Toilets

I discussed in chapter 3 the important role that women's public toilets had historically played in increasing women's ability to participate in public life. Public toilets have since become one of the contested grounds in the clash between women's rights and transgender rights.[40,41] Some managers of public spaces have attempted to sidestep the issue by providing 'gender-neutral' toilets, which are in reality 'mixed-sex' toilets, despite the fact that the provision of mixed-sex-only toilets contravenes Building Regulations guidance,[42] Health and Safety at Work regulations,[43] and underprovision of toilets for women and girls is unlawful under the requirements of the Public Sector Equality Duty of the Equality Act (2010). Furthermore, it is illegal not to provide separate toilets for girls and boys aged eight and over in schools.[44] Even international guidance from the United Nations stipulates separate toilets for girls and boys, and/or women and men.[45]

Globally, it is estimated that over 500 million females (13 per cent of all women in the world) lack access to toilets and sanitation facilities.[46] For both sexes there are health risks such as dysentery, typhoid fever, hepatitis, but the lack of access to toilets creates risks for women and girls that are not present for men and boys, such as toxic shock syndrome, vaginal or urinary infections as well as preventing women from dealing with periods and pregnancy issues with privacy and dignity.

Research conducted in Kenya found a 40 per cent increased risk of sexual assault for women without access to adequate sanitation facilities,[47] with the same research finding a 50 per cent increased risk in India.[48]

Mixed-sex toilets, like unisex changing rooms, increase women's fear and risk of harm and reduce women's access to and use of facilities. Girls were reportedly refusing to use unisex toilets at Scottish secondary schools, such as Jedburgh Grammar and Kelso High School in Scotland, because boys have been waving period products 'like flags' and urinating in period product disposal bins.[49] This is happening at a time where there is increased evidence and awareness of the levels of sexual harassment and assault suffered by girls at schools which is perpetrated by male pupils. The charity End Violence Against Women reported that one in three 6–18-year-old girls say they have experienced unwanted sexual touching at school and 600 rapes in schools were reported to police between 2012 and 2015 – an average of one rape every day of the school year.[50] Increasing young males' access to young females in places where there are rarely adults puts girls at greater risk.

A Freedom of Information request by the *Sunday Times* in 2018 found that just under 90 per cent of complaints of sexual assaults, voyeurism and harassment in changing rooms took place in mixed-sex facilities, and two-thirds of sexual assaults in pools and leisure facilities took place in mixed-sex changing rooms.[51] The argument that transwomen have used women's facilities for years and women have not raised concerns ignores the increased numbers of males identifying as women. In view of the factional support for self-ID, there is also an increased likelihood that predatory men can take advantage of mixed-sex facilities or make false claims of identifying as transgender, while the risk of women feeling uncomfortable with challenging those who appear to be male using female facilities will also rise. With changes in technology, mobile phones and spycams create additional risks, as in the case of Katie Dolatowski, mentioned earlier.

Concerns about toilet provision are not based solely on girls' and women's safety, comfort and dignity, though these are immediately obvious. They also relate to equal access. In her book, *Invisible Women: Exposing data bias in a world designed for men*, writer and campaigner Caroline Criado Perez addresses toilets, amongst many other issues, with specific impacts on women's safety and well-being. She explains that if the decision was made to devote equal space to female and male toilets, women would be disadvantaged. Urinals take up less space than cubicles so more males can use the same space at once. However, even if the decision to allow more space for women were based on this consideration alone, they would still be disadvantaged because of clothing and bodies. Women on average take 2.3 times longer than men to use the toilet.[52] Plus, many women use toilets for dealing with periods and are more likely than men to be accompanied by children. Women need more time and space than men rather than equal provision, based on male patterns and requirements. In addition, some orthodox versions of religions forbid women from using mixed-sex toilets.[53] Where are they supposed to go if only mixed-sex toilets are available in public spaces?

Without single-sex toilets, we're back to the nineteenth century and the 'urinary leash', the restriction of women's movements due to lack of access to toilets. 'We just want to pee'[54] has become another of the phrases used by some in the transgender rights lobby movement to claim that their basic needs are not being met. Women's safety cannot be collateral damage for the fears or risks to males who do not conform to the gender stereotypes associated with their sex. The answer should be found in increasing men's comfort with those who do not present as they do, or third spaces specifically for those with transgender identities. Regardless of our sex, or even gender identity, we all should be able to relatively easily access a safe, clean public toilet when we are outside the home. The problem is that mixed-sex toilets do not meet women's needs. We should keep in mind that the objective of toilets is not to allow us to use them next to people with a purportedly similar self-image – the goal has always been to ensure safety, comfort and dignity. Allowing gender-non-conforming males into female toilets to protect the former from other males makes no sense, since sex-segregated toilets are there for women's safety. Why is the answer to the threat to males of men's violence in male toilets to put women at risk?

Hospital wards and healthcare

NHS guidance issued in 2019 recognised that every patient's right to high-quality care that is safe, effective and respects their privacy and dignity is best served by single-sex wards.[55] Mixed-sex hospital wards were banned in the UK in 2010. Andrew Lansley, who was the UK government's Health Secretary at the time said that new measures to 'name and shame' hospitals that continue to put patients in mixed-sex wards would be introduced, which included strengthening existing fines that primary care trusts could impose on hospitals that breached the rules.[56] In 2017, it was reported that the number of NHS patients being treated on mixed-sex wards had soared, despite the ban, and that in the previous year more than 10,000 patients had been required to share a ward with people of the opposite sex, a rise of 45 per cent on the previous year.[57] The single-sex exceptions permissible under the Equality Act 2010 have identified hospital wards as a space where males who identify as transwomen can be legitimately excluded.

The potential risk to women from male patients is obvious. None of the above prevented NHS Greater Glasgow and Clyde from advising that complaints from women about males with transgender identities in women's hospital wards should be treated as transphobia, and that the woman who complained should be the one who is moved in such circumstances, though they later withdrew the advice after complaints from feminist groups.[58]

Conservative Peer Baroness Nicholson of Winterbourne told the House of Lords in 2022 that a female patient was raped on what was claimed to be a single-sex ward and that when she initially told the police about what had happened, the hospital claimed that her allegation was impossible because the ward was single sex. However, it later transpired that CCTV evidence supported her claim and that the accused was a transgender male. At the time of writing (May 2022), the case is under police investigation. Baroness Nicholson claimed the NHS guidance 'gives priority to trans people over women'.[59]

However, the risk to women's safety in hospital wards goes beyond that posed by patients and extends to staff. Data about male staff demonstrates that female patients are highly vulnerable when in the presence of predatory and abusive males. Ex-nurse Nathan Sutherland was jailed in 2021 for 10 years for raping a woman who was unresponsive and in a coma in a hospital in Phoenix, Arizona. It is believed that he assaulted her multiple times over years and this only came to light because she became pregnant. There have been similar cases in New York in 1996[60] and Argentina[61] in 2015. Stroke patient Valerie Kneale, aged 75, died in hospital in Blackpool, England, in 2018 after being raped in her hospital bed. Healthcare worker Hernando Puno was eventually alleged to have sexually assaulted seven women whilst working in the hospital.[62] In 2020, GP Manish Shah was found to have committed 90 sexual assaults on 24 female patients whom he persuaded to undergo unnecessary intimate examinations.[63] Numerous other doctors, including Frederick Field, David Oliver Burleson, Peter Lieh-Chuan Chi and Dennis Michael Zikowski have been found guilty of similar charges.[64] In 2022, Paul Grayson, from

Sheffield, England, who had worked as a nurse for 25 years, was jailed for 12 years. Grayson had filmed up the gowns of four unconscious women as they recovered from surgery and filmed colleagues using the toilet. There was evidence that he had been filming women since 2012 but he was found guilty of 23 charges which occurred between 2017 and 2020, including 14 charges of voyeurism, three charges of sexual assault, one charge of upskirting, one charge of taking an indecent image of a child, one charge of installing recording equipment for the purposes of sexual gratification and three charges of possessing indecent images of children.[65]

A male nursing assistant Callum Knox was found guilty of assaulting two elderly female patients, Ann Reid and Agnes Ferguson, both aged 81, in a hospital in Ayrshire, Scotland. Both women died, although murder and manslaughter charges against Knox were found unproven.[66] Dr Harold Shipman is recorded as having killed 173 patients but it is believed the total number is higher, around 250, in the UK between 1975 and 1998. Eighty per cent of his victims were elderly women.[67] Meanwhile, concerns about women's mortality in healthcare extend beyond homicide. Research which included 1.3 million patients found that women were 34 per cent more likely to die if treated by a male rather than female surgeon.[68]

A 2018 survey of over 7,000 people found that 46 per cent of women would prefer to be seen by a female doctor, while only 6 per cent preferred to be seen by a male.[69] One study found that 63.2 per cent of sexual misconduct-related reports were made against male nurses, while less than 10 per cent of nurses were male.[70] Another found that two-thirds of the those investigated for boundary violation cases were male, in contrast to the percentage of men in the nursing profession, which was about 9 per cent.[71] A third study found that 77 per cent of sexual offence convictions against nurses which resulted in criminal charges were committed by males, but males represented only 8 per cent of the workforce.[72] A review of research records, which included 32 reports covering over four million cases of poor performance, found that male doctors had nearly two and a half times the odds of being subject to medical legal action than female doctors.[73] Finally, a study which asked whether there was evidence of 'gender-related' bias in allegations of misconduct or the application of disciplinary procedures found no evidence of such bias.[74] In other words, research has consistently found that male medical staff are disproportionately represented in those facing malpractice complaints and procedures. It's worth remembering, with the proviso that their research was looking at violent offending rather than medical malpractice (but also that there is a gap in the research comparing the prevalence of behaviours between those males or females with transgender identities and those without), that the research by Dhejne et al. found that violent offending in males with transgender identities followed the same pattern as that of other males.[75] My concern about males with transgender identities is not that they are transgender, but that they are males.

Meanwhile, the idea of widespread female-only – staff and patients – healthcare seems like an impossible dream. However, in Australia, the Illawara Women's Trauma Recovery Centre, in Wollongong, New South Wales, provides free or low-cost and affordable medical, allied and complementary healthcare.[76] All staff are female. Their website states 'We operate from a feminist perspective. This means we understand and value women's life experiences and recognise the continued discrimination and structural inequality they face in their communities and Australian society.'[77] Also in Australia, in 2021, The Lisa Thurin Women's Mental Health Centre was opened in Wollongong, New South Wales, by Cabrini, a large not-for-profit Catholic healthcare service provider. Sharon Sherwood, Cabrini's chief of mental health and outreach services, said 'A lot of women don't get help because the thought of having to go into a shared mental health space makes them feel unsafe.'

Referring to mixed-sex mental health hospitals, she said 'They're violent places, as a . . . female who has an addiction problem or is suffering from PTSD or some kind of complex trauma, do you really want to put yourself in that situation to get better? They're not trauma-informed environments.'[78]

If we cannot replicate women-only healthcare across the globe, across all women's healthcare needs, we can and should at least hear, acknowledge and act upon women's fears and concerns, and be aware of the risks that males pose. Unlike in refuges where we can create and maintain women-only spaces, risk assessment addressing the risks posed by males – as patients and as staff – must be undertaken and risk mitigation steps implemented.

Feminist campaigner Jean Hatchet told me,

When I had been taken to hospital by police after being attacked in the street by my abuser, I was terrified and needed support. A male nurse was allowed into the room alone. He began berating me for not giving my name and address to the doctor, calling me selfish and stupid. I gathered my things and left the hospital ward when no one was looking. Male staff shouldn't be around women in that state. I needed a woman to help me understand. To treat me sensitively. Not to make me more frightened than I was.

Women victim-survivors of men's violence have health issues outside of those directly related to the abuse perpetrated upon them. Jean has stage three (advanced) cancer, and it has spread to secondary sites in her body. She told me,

When I had extensive cyto-reductive surgery for ovarian cancer, it wasn't certain I would survive it. On the gynae ward were other women in for similar. Recovery was hard, with self-administered morphine drips leaving us vulnerable and semi-conscious. I found it incredibly hard as a survivor of sexual and domestic abuse to have male cleaners on the ward even for brief periods. It would have been agonising and intolerable to have a male-bodied person on that ward in a bed close by. I know I would not have allowed myself the pain relief I badly needed. I would have stayed alert. My past experience would have told me to be wary.

Healthcare staffing goes beyond doctors and nurses too, and often takes place in someone's home as well as a hospital setting. If males with transgender identities can be employed as if they were women in health and social care, can a female refuse help with intimate care like washing and using the toilet (whether this happens in her home or a ward) from a male in the safe knowledge that a female will be assigned to her case?

It is important to say that most who work in health and social care are highly professional, respect boundaries and want to do the best for those they care for. However, more than a quarter of women in the world have been subjected to physical or sexual, or both, intimate partner violence in their lifetime,[79] so my concerns are about patient needs. Many women will have a very different experience of healthcare if that care is provided by a male, no matter how competent and compassionate he is. Research has also shown that women who have been subjected to sexual assault are more likely to have a stroke and heart disease,[80] twice as likely to develop breast cancer (odds ratio 2.21) with multiple exposure to sexual assault carrying a two- to three-fold increased risk compared with a single episode.[81] In other words, the prevalence of men's violence against women and girls should be reason enough for medical care to be trauma-informed and one of the ways of providing this is to offer single-sex spaces.

Women's bodies – only women bleed

The cervix is a female body part, an internal part of a woman's reproductive organs. It is a neck of fibromuscular tissue connecting the vagina and the womb/uterus. It has a small opening allowing shedded endometrium lining (menstrual blood) to leave the body and semen to enter the womb.

In June 2017, Edward Morris, Vice President of the Royal College of Obstetricians and Gynaecologists, wrote about research which had found out that 43 per cent of women were unable to identify the cervix as the neck of the womb.[82] Despite this, in the summer of 2018, Cancer Research UK dropped the word 'woman' from its smear test campaign, replacing it with 'everyone with a cervix'.[83] They said this was an attempt to use more inclusive language and not to exclude those who were biologically female but who identified as something else. This is an example of the erasure of our understanding of 'woman' as a sex class. At the time, uptake of cervical screening [smear tests] was at a 20-year low and concerns were expressed about accessibility of language, many pointing out that particularly for those who do not speak English as a first language, such a move might hinder rather than encourage screening. Those who are biologically female but who do not identify as such will be keenly aware that, like it or not, they have female reproductive organs and understand that they are included in messaging about medical issues.

This issue has since extended to period products, tampons and towels. In 2020, Tampax US tweeted 'Fact: Not all women have periods. Also a fact: Not all people with periods are women. Let's celebrate the diversity of all people who bleed! #mythbusting #periodtruths #transisbeautiful.'[84] Tampax, part of Proctor and Gamble, own 29 per cent of the global market share of tampons. The trend to ignore the links of women's bodily functions to women's bodies extends from a global conglomerate with an annual income of over US$13 billion in 2021 ($13,866,000,000 or £10,256,056,230)[85] to a small charity with an annual income of under £500,000. Bloody Good Period, whose campaign for menstrual products for refugees and asylum seekers, describes these people, their beneficiaries, not as women, but as 'people who bleed'.[86] Their guide to language claims that when talking about periods, referring solely to females should be avoided because some people who have periods do not identify as women and that everyone deserves to be included.[87]

Trans rights activist Munroe Bergdorf claimed that the 'pussy hats' worn by some women attending women's marches, particularly in the US in 2017, were reductive and exclusionary because they centred on [women's] reproductive systems. The knitted hats had cat-like ears, a play on the slang word pussy to refer to vulvas, and symbolised women's objections to then US President Donald Trump's remark in 2005 that he would 'grab 'em [women] by the pussy'. According to Bergdorf, women who recognise the vulva as a symbol of the universality of women's oppression, are getting feminism wrong, pushing out those (transwomen) who do not have them.[88]

Bergdorf claimed that the hats reduced women to 'walking vaginas',[89] misusing the central feminist position that women are more than our body parts. Of course we are. The feminist position is that women's bodies should not and need not define the entirety or scope of women's lives, that our sex and socially prescribed sex roles are not the same. This is far from saying that we do not share the material reality of a sexed body.[90]

The British Pregnancy Advisory Service (BPAS), the UK's leading abortion care service, was criticised for using the word woman in their material.[91] Although they had acknowledged their services, advocacy and campaigning are inclusive of (female) trans, non-binary and intersex people, BPAS stood their ground:

> . . . we will also continue to use the word 'women' over 'people' so we can continue to campaign effectively for reproductive

rights. Women's reproductive healthcare and choices remain regulated and restricted in the way they are precisely because they are women's issues, sadly still bound up with heavily gendered and judgmental approaches to female sexuality, ideals of motherhood and expectations of maternal sacrifice, and the need to control women's bodies and choices. If we cannot clearly articulate that it is predominantly women, rather than people at large, who are affected by this we will find it much harder to dismantle a framework that today is still underpinned by sexism, and achieve a broader goal of ensuring that everyone, no matter how they identify, can access the care and support they need as swiftly and straightforwardly as possible.[92]

Research has supported the stance taken by BPAS and called for clarity in terminology and avoiding conflation of terms, arguing that there are significant implications to de-sexing language when referring to inherently sexed processes and states. Whilst recognising the need to be inclusive and respectful, it has been argued that

> Those who do not identify as women or mothers, and yet become pregnant and give birth, are most benefited by a culture and health service that recognises and deeply understands the underlying molecular, cellular, behavioral and organismal aspects required to reproduce.[93]

Perhaps, then, it should not be surprising that some men appear to be terribly confused about the difference between a vulva, a vagina and a cervix. The woeful level of knowledge was exposed by presenter Piers Morgan, who, in 2021, had responded with scorn to a tweet by news channel CNN stating that, according to the American Cancer Society, individuals with a cervix are now recommended to start cervical cancer screening at 25 years of age. His answer: 'Do you mean women?'[94]

Labour MP for Canterbury, Rosie Duffield, liked Morgan's tweet and in doing so sparked a markedly hostile reaction from transgender activists online, later saying that the level of vitriol had left her 'completely terrified'.[95] However, she responded not with an apology and the desired level of contrition, but with a defiant 'I'm a "transphobe" for knowing that only women have a cervix?!'[96] Duffield continued to be a subject of the activists' ire and was advised not to attend the Labour Party Annual Conference that year for her own safety.[97] Labour leader, Keir Starmer, when asked the question 'Is it transphobic to say that only women have a cervix?' by the BBC's Andrew Marr, responded with 'It is something that shouldn't be said. It is something that is not right.'[98] MP Emily Thornberry, when asked a similar question, responded by replying that her cousin, a trans man (and therefore biologically female) was a man and had a cervix.[99]

Two days later, at a Labour Party conference fringe group meeting, David Lammy described women, usually politically on the right, but some in the Labour Party too, as 'dinosaurs' who wanted to 'hoard rights'. The following day, LBC radio presenter Nick Ferrari asked MP David Lammy whether it was transphobic to say that only women have cervixes. Lammy's reply 'I don't know whether it's transphobic, but it's not accurate, Nick. I mean, obviously, it's probably the case that only, that transwomen don't have ovaries, but a cervix, I understand, is something that you can have, er, following various procedures and hormone treatment and all the rest of it.'[100]

Perhaps one might be inclined to be sympathetic to the confusion suffered by politicians when we learn that medical students at Napier University in Edinburgh, Scotland were taught in an online module that biological males could become pregnant and so instructions on how to catheterise a male 'birthing person' were given. It transpired that the member of staff who updated existing material had confused a transman, a female with a masculine transgender identity, with a biological male. An email contained the following: 'This update was made to take account of the fact that while most times the birthing person will have female genitalia, you may be caring for a pregnant or birthing person which is transitioning from male to female and may still have external male genitalia.' This of course is not possible. Equally worryingly, a representative of campaign groups Sex Not Gender Midwives expressed concern about the culture of fear which prevented students from raising questions at their university.[101]

Females are, from birth, expected to one day either bear children, decide not to bear them or deal with the consequences of female infertility. Female children are raised accordingly, with these three paths influencing how others engage with them. The percentage of women who remained childfree has remained fairly consistent since the late 1950s, with just over 80 per cent of women having at least one child by the end of their childbearing years in 2020. Whether women have children or not, these paths carry great material and social consequences. Males do not face these consequences in the same way.

The resistance to removing the word woman from descriptions of our biology and anatomy must not mean a denial of the needs of males or females with transgender identities nor a lack of respect for their dignity. Serious health risks occur if a person receives medical treatment based on their gender identity and not their sex; that is, if they were assumed to be the sex that they are not and treated accordingly. A solution could be for sex and gender identity to both be recorded for those who desire it.[102,103] However, this does open risks of mistakes in emergency situations, which will need to be addressed. In some situations, the option of third or fourth spaces could be explored and staff should be appropriately trained to consider all people's needs, transgender or not.

Female individuals with transgender identities (transmen) can become pregnant and have periods. Breastfeeding may be possible in some females who have had some form of masculinisation surgery but it is very difficult or not possible for others, in part according to the method of surgery and the lack of tissue or sufficient skin. There are concerns that lactation and breastfeeding may be distressing for some transmen, alongside other concerns about stigmatising and pathologising attitudes from healthcare staff and other members of the public. There is evidence that oestrogen therapy can be combined with additional drugs (spironolactone, cyproterone acetate and gonadotropin-releasing hormone agonists) to induce lactation in males. However, the American Food and Drug Administration warns that the use of domperidone to stimulate milk production poses 'unknown risks to infants'.[104] As the population of transgender people grows, increasing numbers will be having families. There have been claims that transmen have an increased prevalence of polycystic ovary syndrome (PCOS) compared with other females and PCOS is associated with a higher risk of other health problems. Research appears to show that this is not as a result of hormone treatment but that the prevalence of PCOS is higher in transmen in the first place.[105,106] Leading on from this, as Parker Hurley explained 'When it comes to taking care of body parts that many of us would like to ignore altogether, like our ovaries, we have an even greater tendency to avoid routine healthcare and screenings.'[107] It is important that health and care support is appropriate, and that barriers to access for people with transgender identities are addressed to meet the physical and physiological needs of all involved.

However, males who have undergone genital surgery do not have a cervix. They don't have a womb with endometrium lining to shed. Males do not have periods. If sperm enters their surgically created orifice, there is no route for it to take towards insemination. Males who have undergone genital surgery do not have a vagina or a vulva. Males do not get pregnant. They do not require access to abortions. Males do not give birth. It is not only women's spaces that we need to defend, but our ability to talk about the functioning of our own bodies.

Feminist conferences and meetings

The need to defend our women-only spaces, our spaces of solidarity, growth, sharing, learning, celebration and healing across our many differences suggests that those spaces are a threat, since our resistance to subjugation does not please some males. Through what we can achieve through women-only spaces, we are a challenge to male supremacy.

In 2012, feminist activist Julia Long and others organised a radical feminism conference in London, RadFem 2012, at which I was a speaker.[108] Naturally, the conference was open to females only, but in response to complaints about inclusivity, the venue, Conway Hall, cancelled the booking. In a piece published in the *Guardian*, trans rights activist Roz Kaveney had opined that radical feminism paid no regard to choice or preference, the standard neo-liberal arguments used to excuse the sexual exploitation of women, which Kaveney had also mentioned.[109] In an example of balance which is rarely seen today, *The Guardian* also published a piece in response by Sheila Jeffreys, a speaker at the conference. Defending feminists' right to discuss transgender issues, Jeffreys wrote

> the recent increased identification of children as transgender, the phenomenon of transgender regrets, that is those persons who consider they have made a mistake. Given that the drug and surgical treatments have now been normalised and are increasingly embarked upon by young lesbians and sought out by parents for young children, it is most important that the rights of researchers and theorists to comment and investigate should be protected.[110]

Ten years later, Jeffreys' concerns have only proven to be apposite.

The conference was the first UK feminist event that I am aware of which was targeted by trans rights activists' attempts to close it down, to prevent women from gathering and discussing issues which affect us. The following year, RadFem 2013, originally booked at London Irish Centre, was held at the Camden Centre after activists bullied employees of the Irish Centre, including with telephone calls threatening violence.[111]

In 2018, Venice Allen organised a conference room at Millwall Football Club's stadium to discuss proposed changes to the GRA. Despite Millwall having a reputation of being a tough football club, they could not withstand the harassment of the activists trying to prevent the event from happening and cancelled the booking.[112] Undeterred, Allen booked the event at a new venue: The House of Commons.

At the Vancouver Women's Library launch in 2017, a group called Gays Against Gentrification crashed the party and intimidated women attendees: they poured wine on books, tore down posters and set off the fire alarm. The protesters accused the women of being 'SWERFs'[113] and 'TERFs'. Unfortunately, the library only survived a few years before being forced to close because the protests and backlash made it very difficult to sustain.[114]

In April 2018, in Hendon Magistrates Court, North London, Tara Wolf, a 26-year-old white male who identifies as transgender, was found guilty of assault by beating a 60-year-old woman, Maria MacLachlan.[115] Just over 6 months earlier, in September 2017, MacLachlan had been with other women at Speakers Corner, Hyde Park, waiting to attend a talk on proposed changes to the GRA. In court, Wolf admitted to posting 'I wanna f*** up some terfs. They're no better than fash' on Facebook before turning up to protest the event. At Wolf's trial, Judge Kenneth Grant insisted that MacLachlan, the victim of the assault, use the female pronouns 'she' and 'her' to refer to her attacker as a matter of courtesy. Although Wolf was ordered to pay a £150 fine, a surcharge of £30 and £250 costs, Judge Grant refused to award criminal injuries compensation to MacLachlan, who had been left with facial bruising, grazed knees and red marks on her neck, as well as insomnia and a fear of large crowds. The judge described MacLachlan's reference to her attacker as 'he' when describing the assault as ungraceful, and one of the reasons for failing to award compensation.[116]

Julie Bindel is a journalist and feminist activist who has spent her adult life fighting for women's rights and against men's violence against women. Julie is also a passionate fighter for the abolition of prostitution. In 2019, after having spoken at an event in Edinburgh, she was lunged at and verbally abused by trans rights activist Cathy Brennan who was later charged with breach of the peace. In Scotland, a breach of the peace charge can be made when a person engages in conduct 'severe enough to cause alarm to ordinary people and threaten serious disturbance to the community'. On Twitter, Brennan admitted to calling Julie 'a TERF cunt'.[117] It took three security guards to keep Brennan away from her. Julie said, 'I have been beaten up by men in the past but not for a long time, and I knew precisely what was coming when I saw the rage on his face.'[118]

The tactic of attempting to prevent women from meeting to discuss and organise against sexual oppression has become well established and has extended beyond women-only gatherings to any with a feminist theme or which address issues of concern to women, especially debates over the importance of biological sex and the Gender Recognition Act. Since the efforts to stop the 2012 and 2013 RadFem conferences, several Woman's Place UK meetings have had to change venues, sometimes on the actual day of the meeting because confirmed venues have been intimidated into cancelling. These one-sided attempts at censorship are not happening in reverse. Feminists have not tried to prevent transgender people from holding meetings. It is wrong to claim that changes to the GRA or transgender identity ideology are matters of concern only for people who identify as transgender. As I am showing throughout this book, changes to the GRA, especially self-identification, could have serious implications for women and women-only spaces, so it is right that they should be considered at feminist gatherings.

As yet, no meeting has been prevented from taking place, which, given the scale of efforts to shut them down, is a testimony to women's power of resistance. Demonstrations are now simply expected outside feminist meetings, sometimes noisy chanting or seeking to drown out the voices of women talking about violence that men have done to them.

Women continue to meet, discuss, strategise, share and celebrate. The fact that males and, sadly, some women who support them, find this objectionable, speaks volumes.

Women's prizes

Worldwide, women and girls are hugely under-represented in politics, science, academia and the arts. According to the United Nations, in 2020, globally, women comprised 25 per cent of parliamentarians, women made up 6.6 per cent of the number of CEOs in the Fortune 500, and of 900 Nobel Prize winners, only 53 were women.[119] In 93 years of the Oscars, and 462 nominated films, only seven women (in eight nominations, with two nominations for Jane Campion) have been nominated for Best Director[120] and just 4 per cent of chefs who hold three Michelin stars were women.[121]

Women's prizes developed because women's contributions are often overlooked and also to help address the under-representation of women in some fields. As with women-only spaces, there have been criticisms that women's prizes are sexist, rather than an attempt to tackle sexism.

Since its inception in 1969, 33 males and 19 females have won the Booker Prize for fiction. However, sexism goes deeper than who wins the prize. Nishtha Madaan investigated stereotypes in the adjectives and verbs associated with male and female characters in books that had been shortlisted for the prize. She found that men were more likely than women to be depicted in positions of power while women were more likely to be assigned more submissive roles, with female characters mentioned 50 per cent less than males. Meanwhile, of 114 awards of the Nobel Prize in literature, just 14 had been awarded to women, and 19 of 69 awards of the Pulitzer Prize in Fiction have been given to women.[122]

Transgender males are increasingly being nominated for women's awards. Phillip Bunce, a self-described 'proud father and husband' who sometimes wears women's clothes and uses the name Pippa, was, in 2018 ranked thirty-second in a list of Britain's top 100 female executives compiled for the Champions of Women in Business awards.[123]

In 2015, transgender former athlete Caitlin Jenner was named as one of BBC Radio Four Woman's Hour top ten (women) influencers, supposedly women who have had 'an exceptionally large impact'.[124] Later that year, in a Buzzfeed article, Jenner piled insult on injury, claiming that 'the hardest part about being a woman is figuring out what to wear'.[125] In 2021, trans author Torrey Peters was longlisted for the Women's Prize for Fiction, after it had been agreed that the prize was open to anyone who was a 'cis woman, or a transgender woman who is legally defined as a woman'.[126] A transwoman, Mj Rodrigues, won the 2021 Golden Globe award for best actress. In 2022, a transgender barrister, Robin White, was shortlisted for 'leader of the year' of the Women Influence and Power in Law UK Awards, a legal profession award.[127] The Brazilian edition of *Marie Claire* in December 2021 named Indianara Siqueira, as one of seven women making a difference for human rights[128] despite accusations regarding sexual exploitation, including of minors, and other unethical behaviours and activities which led to Siqueira being expelled from the Socialism and Liberty Party.[129]

In 2014, *New York Magazine* identified Martine Rothblatt as the highest paid female CEO in America. Except Rothblatt, lawyer and pharmaceutical business millionaire, who was on the front cover as a result of this accolade, is male. Responding to the accolade, Rothblatt said 'I can't claim that what I have achieved is equivalent to what a woman has achieved. For the first half of my life, I was male.'[130] Of course, even while identifying as a woman during the second half of life, Rothblatt remains male.

And whilst males are being awarded prizes or celebrated for excellence in the fields supposedly to recognise women, some trans activists try to block women whose contribution has been identified as worthy of merit. Back in 2008, when Stonewall was an organisation representing lesbians, gay men and bisexual people, Julie Bindel had been nominated for Journalist of the Year in Stonewall's annual awards. When Julie turned up at the event she was greeted by a large mob of transgender activists and supporters shouting 'no platform for bigotry'. Their objection was based on a piece that Julie had written (in 2004) looking at diagnosis of transsexuality as being based on outmoded sex stereotypes. The Journalist of the Year award was supposedly decided by public vote. Julie didn't win but later learned that she had received twice the number of votes as the woman who was declared winner.[131]

Each time a male is included in the shortlist for a prize created to address the marginalisation of women, a woman is prevented from being shortlisted, recognised or winning. This cannot be deemed progress. It is of course laudable that individuals who identify as transgender are recognised for the excellence of their contributions in their chosen fields, but I would prefer that their recognition did not come at the expense of members of the oppressed sex.

Women's sports

National and international sports governing bodies have been opening women's sports to males with transgender identities despite evidence which demonstrates that males, regardless of transition, retain meaningful physical advantages in comparison to females. Again, in my opinion, inclusion of males with transgender identities has been prioritised over fairness and, in some sports – notably martial arts, boxing, wrestling – women's safety. While the decision to prevent males who identify as transwomen from competing with women in World Rugby[132] has not been adopted in the UK by the Rugby Football Union, testosterone level limits have been introduced[133] and checks on height and weight proposed.[134]

Transgender athletes who have won or entered women's sports at elite levels include Canadian cyclist Rachel McKinnon (now Veronica Ivy), who twice qualified as the world champion of women's cycling, winning the Masters Track Cycling World Championship in 2018 and 2019 after transitioning at the age of 29.[135] Meanwhile, Laurel Hubbard competed in the 2020 Summer Olympics held in 2021 and, at 43, was the fourth oldest athlete to ever compete at the Olympics and the oldest weightlifter to qualify. Hubbard had been lifting weights since being a teenager. In 2012, aged 34 Hubbard transitioned. In 2017, aged 39, Hubbard competed in international weightlifting for the first time.[136] Amongst males of the same weight, Hubbard would not be good enough to be lifting weights in the Olympics. In 2021 and 2022, 22-year-old transgender swimmer Lia Thomas was winning national women's swimming competitions. Lia had formerly competed with men under the name Will Thomas and had been placed 554th in the 200 metres race. In addition, Thomas's female teammates have shared their discomfort[137] that they are required to share changing and showering space with Lia Thomas, who has had hormonal treatment[138] but has neither confirmed nor denied having genital surgery and, in any case, continues to benefit from having experienced male puberty. Andraya Yearwood is a sprinter, who, in 2017, won the Connecticut state title. In 2018 Andraya was pushed into second place by another transgender sprinter, Terry Miller. The first female to finish achieved only third place.[139]

In June 2022, a 29-year-old male, Ricci Tres, claimed first place in the Boardr street skating (skateboarding) contest in New York. The competition is open to everyone, but the heats and finals are split according to gender and therefore remain mixed sex. A 13-year-old girl, Shiloh Catori, came second and a 16-year-old girl, Jordan Pascale, came third.[140] Tres, a father of three, had said, 'I know I will never be a woman.'[141] Nevertheless, in 2021, Tres had tried to participate in the Women's Street USA Skateboarding National Championships as a stepping stone to competing in the Olympics, but had been rejected due to high testosterone levels.[142] In 2021, transgender skateboarder Lillian Gallagher had won the Red Bull Cornerstone women's skating competition. The woman beaten into second place, Taylor Silverman, later wrote to Red Bull voicing her concerns. Silverman pointed out that biological males have a clear advantage and said she believed 'in doing the right thing, even if it is not the popular thing'.[143] Red Bull permitted males to compete in women's skateboarding divisions despite having published a blog in 2016 which said, 'The group of muscles in the abdominal region, the obliques and part of the back, play a pivotal role in skateboarding performance.'[144] Males who have gone through puberty tend to have larger oblique back muscles. Journalist and skateboarder Tim Pool commented, 'Males in skateboarding have higher centers of gravity, granting advantages that cannot be removed with hrt. That plus the Q angle differences. So it's unfair to female athletes.'[145]

In 2019, developmental biologist Emma Hilton spoke at a conference held jointly by Women's Place UK and Fair Play For Women about the participation of male transgender

athletes in women's sports, along with former Olympic
swimmer Sharron Davies and Victoria Hood, track/road
race cyclist and manager of the Jadan-Weldtite Vive le Velo
women's race team.[146] Hilton cited academic research looking at musculoskeletal changes in transwomen suppressing
testosterone, which concluded that the resulting loss of
muscle mass and strength is small, that strength advantage
over females is retained and went on to inform the audience
that male transgender competitors retain stiffer connective
tissue – ligaments and tendons – which mean greater stor-
age of energy and power. Males have larger muscles, hearts,
lungs and haemoglobin pools, all of which provide sporting
advantages. Hilton, who is a research associate specialising
in Cellular & Developmental Systems as well as Evolution,
Systems and Genomics, said that such a list was the tip of an
iceberg of '6,500 differences in gene expression between males
and females', with 'many unknowns that science has still to
fathom'.[147] The body of research that shows that males with
transgender identities retain physical advantages over women
in sports continues to grow.[148,149] Female former elite athletes
are increasingly adding their voices to those of women like
Davies and Hood to defend women's sports.[150]

Women's sport is still the poor relation, drawing in less
money, usually offering lower value prizes, attracting lower
audiences. We are far from reaching equality of the sexes in
sport, though in the UK we are seeing the growth in popular-
ity of women's football, cricket and rugby. The inclusion of
transgender males in women's sports risks pushing women's
sport further back into the shadows.

Even where transwomen fail to win, such as Laurel Hubbard
in the 2020 Olympics, a female athlete has been prevented
from competing. And it's not just elite sports where males with
transgender identities are affecting women's participation.
A woman who is a Muslim feminist with a very long history
of challenging religious fundamentalism and men's violence

against women, and who requires anonymity because of the possible risks to her employment, told me

> There has been much campaigning by Black women's groups aligning themselves with trans rights activists and an equating of racism with discrimination against transmen and transwomen. However, what has not been discussed is what is happening to minoritised women in their communities as a result of the trans debate. In researching the growth in religious fundamentalisms in minoritised communities, several women disclosed to me that they were no longer able to access services/activities that were once women-only spaces. Women-only swimming sessions were cited as now being off limits, as these were no longer women-only, since men could attend the sessions, access the changing rooms, etc., if they simply said they were women. I asked at my local authority swimming pool about women-only sessions and take up of these sessions – I was told that 'very few Muslim women now attend' but was not provided with reasons for this.

In Chicago, Illinois, in 2017, an 18-year-old male won a two-year battle to change in the girl's changing room. Nova Maday had been provided with a private cubicle in which to change but claimed that that constituted discrimination. A female student, Julia Burca, fought back the tears as she explained that as a swimmer, she had to change 'multiple times, naked, in front of the other students in the locker room'. And that she felt 'uncomfortable that [her] privacy is being invaded'.[151]

Girl Guides

Helen Watts was involved with the Girl Guides from the age of 7 until she was 33, when she was sacked from her position as unit leader in 2018 due to her raising concerns about safeguarding over the inclusion of males with transgender identities and also potential blocks to parental consent. Katie Alcock, a woman who shared these views, faced similar treatment. In a blog published by Woman's Place UK, Helen described how Girl Guides formed a relationship with Gendered Intelligence in 2016 and then, in 2017, changed their policy from being an all-female group to one which was inclusive of self-identified women and girls. She said, 'under the new policy self-identified women and girls who are biologically and legally male are treated the same in terms of safeguarding and privacy (e.g., shared accommodation on residential trips) as female children and leaders'. Recognising the safeguarding risks here, she continues: 'Girls from other protected groups could be put off joining altogether, even to the point of indirect discrimination. A disabled girl may be less inclined to join if she is not guaranteed a female for medical or personal care; girls from minority faith groups may not want to join if males are present.'[152] In 2022, Katie Alcock released a statement saying that she had reached a resolution with Girlguiding. The organisation stated that it recognised that sex and gender were not the same and furthermore that the safeguarding of girls would always be at the heart of everything they did. Nevertheless, the organisation reiterated that membership of their 'girl-only' charity was open to those who were biologically female and also to those who were subject to the protected characteristic of gender reassignment.[153]

Sexual objectification and the performance of femininity

Identifying and resisting the sexual objectification of women is a basic feminist objective. Jenny Fortune, Sarah Wilson and Sally Alexander were amongst the women who protested the

Miss World beauty contest in 1970.[154] Women, from veteran campaigner Clare Short (MP for Birmingham Ladywood from 1983 to 2010) to the now disbanded campaign group 'No More Page Three', rallied against the insidious practice of the right-wing tabloid *The Sun* hosting a large image of a topless young woman on its page three from 1970 to 2015, when it finally ceased. But the *Sunday Sport* was still publishing images of topless women in 2022.[155,156,157]

Feminists know that, as long as women are seen and judged as decorative objects, reduced to body parts, judged by sexist beauty standards and simultaneously as men's possessions, women will be seen as 'less than', functioning to serve men, either literally or for their pleasure. Whilst I recognise that the latter is a generalisation and certainly not applicable to all women, John Berger wrote

> Men look at women. Women watch themselves being looked at. This determines not only most relations between men and women but also the relation of women to themselves. The surveyor of woman in herself is male: the surveyed female. Thus she turns herself into an object – and most particularly an object of vision: a sight.[158]

This was further developed by Laura Mulvey[159] who coined the term 'male gaze', denoting how women are seen and valued from the perspective of heterosexual men as objects framed by male desire (or not). Thus, women are socialised to view and rate ourselves through the male gaze. Feminism challenges this patriarchal socialised practice, reminding us that women are subjects, not objects, and that our value will not be reduced to how we are judged by heteropatriarchal beauty standards. It is striking how often many women enjoying a woman-only space for the first time experience joy that they were not expecting when freed of this often-subconscious habit. Women who have attend FILIA conferences regularly express this in their feedback to the conference organisers. Kruti Walsh told me:

> I started going to nightclubs when I was 15. It was common for girls and women to be grinded on, groped and touched without their consent. I had low self-esteem and was naive enough to think this was normal and even to be flattered by the attention. As I got older I became more aware of the dangers of sexual assault and spiking. I was even thrown out of a club for threatening to punch a man who groped me.
>
> When I went to Todmorden women's disco for the first time in my early 30s, the first thing I noticed was how happy and comfortable all the women looked. Many were in comfortable clothes, flat shoes and minimal or no make-up. Away from the male gaze and the dress codes of patriarchal institutions, there's no need for women to subject themselves to revealing clothes, tottering heels and heavy make-up – unless they want to! The real revelation, though, came when I hit the dancefloor. I felt so free and so liberated, I danced with my eyes closed for the first time. It was an incredible feeling. I knew I was safe, that no man could grope me or grind on me. I could dance with my eyes closed, in the way I wanted to, connected to and moved by the music – not having to put on a show and dance in the way I'd been conditioned to. I had an exhilarating time that night, dancing and laughing with my sisters. I'd have loved to go again and again but I couldn't find any women-only clubs in London (where I live). At least we have the FiLiA party, once a year.[160]

Sexual objectification is an expression of power and femininity is the uniform of subjugation. I write this with full awareness that compliance with many of the socially acceptable standards of femininity is an accusation that can be fairly made of me. My Faustian Pact buys me a pass in heteropatriarchal society denied of women who do not comply. It is true that there is no shortage of women who celebrate sexual objectification, who habitually compete with other women to gain male approval, value themselves through the distortive reflection of the male gaze and perform femininity. This is because women have been socialised to do so, and although some women do consciously unpick and desist, the churn of women engaged in this destructive practice is no reason for feminists to deny that the acceptance or celebration of objectification is harmful. Others (usually men) claim that objectification bestows a power upon women over men.[161] An ideology is most effective if its oppressed class does its bidding, accepts it as normal and even polices compliance.

Whilst I must make the proviso that this doesn't apply to all, we frequently see the celebration of objectification in transwomen. Paris Lees, a journalist who is trans wrote, 'I was catcalled, sexually objectified and treated like a piece of meat by men the entire week. And it was absolutely awesome.'[162] And in the same piece claimed to 'struggle to see any real connection between rape and the guy who wolf-whistled at me this morning'. As I've mentioned before, Liz Kelly used the concept of the 'continuum of sexual violence' more than 30 years ago, to describe the links across the range of forms of men's violence against and abuse of women, and street harassment, or wolf-whistles, belong on that continuum. Leyna Bloom, a trans model, on the occasion of being the first transwoman to feature on the cover of the annual *Sports Illustrated* swimsuit issue, said 'This moment heals a lot of pain in the world. We deserve this moment; we have waited millions of years to show up as survivors and be seen as full humans filled with wonder.'[163] Bloom failed to understand that sexual objectification is the antithesis of being seen as fully human. Trans writer Grace Lavery took things a step further, laying bare that validation was more important than the status or even treatment of women, and stated:

> There is something about being treated like shit by men that feels like affirmation itself, like a cry of delight from the deepest

cavern of my breast. . . . To be the victim of honest, undisguised sexism possesses an exhilarating vitality.[164]

Lesbians and same-sex attraction

Like Stonewall, the National Centre for Lesbian Rights in the USA is inclusive of males with transgender identities and describes itself as 'leading advocate for the rights of transgender youth';[165] the same goes for Egale Canada and PFLAG (Parents and Friends of Lesbians and Gays) Canada, GAYrus sia.ru, the National LGBTI Health Alliance in Australia, Pink Dot in Singapore, the Blue Diamond Society in Nepal, J-FLAG in Jamaica, the Gay and Lesbian Coalition of Kenya, Helem in Lebanon, Solidarity for LGBT Human Rights of Korea and many others basing their beneficiary groups on sexuality and advancing equality and justice for lesbian, gay, bisexual people and into gender identities.

In 2021, the Tasmanian Anti-Discrimination Commissioner, Sarah Bolt, refused to grant an exemption to allow Lesbian, Gay and Bisexual Alliance Australia to exclude males from their lesbian events, ruling that the exclusion of transwomen carried a 'significant risk' of breaching legislation. Jessica Hoyle, who lodged the request for a single sex exemption, launched a fundraiser in 2022 to finance an appeal which may be heard in the High Court. The case has the potential to become an Australian national test case and make it unlawful for lesbians to exclude males from lesbian public social events. Hoyle told *The Australian*, 'Many lesbians feel uncomfortable having [them] in their spaces, because they are not female; they are biological males . . . We are forced to have them in our groups but none of us want to date them . . . I feel discriminated against by Sarah Bolt on the basis of being a lesbian same-sex-attracted (woman).'[166,167]

Whilst not true of all, there seems to be no space that some males with transgender identities respect as female-only, even lesbianism, others recognise and reject this coercion and accept that lesbians are same sex-attracted. Many trans people and trans rights advocates condemn the judgement cast on those who insist that their lesbian attraction can only be sex-based. They accept that many, perhaps most lesbians will only be attracted to other females. Nevertheless, there appears to be increasing pressure on lesbians to renounce same-sex attraction in favour of same-gender attractions. The concept of the 'cotton ceiling' was adapted from the term 'glass ceiling' to reflect a lack of sexual access to lesbians from males who identified as lesbians, referring to the barrier to getting inside their knickers. Others claim that the concept of sexuality is changing, that it is losing its currency and that there is increased 'fluidity' in younger people. To many, including me, this sounds like bisexuality. However, if one accepts the concept of bisexuality, you are accepting that there are two sexes; and, as is clear, this is contested by some. Lesbian researcher Angela Wild reported that lesbian dating sites are now regularly used by males, with many lesbians now finding them unusable. Kathleen Stock informed BBC Woman's Hour in 2021 of 'going onto lesbian dating sites and seeing males' and went on to describe 'real pressure on lesbians to accept that trans women can be lesbians' and friends who had been pressured into dating transwomen'.[168] Wild also found high levels of sexual violence against lesbians perpetrated by males who identified as transwomen and claimed to be lesbians. Wild's study was of a small self-selecting sample (with 80 respondents, of whom just under half were UK-based) and so we cannot make conclusions about general prevalence in the UK or elsewhere. However, hers was a qualitative and not a quantitative piece of research and whilst we must maintain consistent standards of critique, Wild made no claims to extend any statistical findings in her research beyond the study's respondents. Lesbian barrister and former fire-fighter Lucy Masoud said that she has seen males who identify as transwomen 'prey on young girls as young as 14 years old' and 'bully' and 'coerce' them into relationships, describing this as 'sinister' and 'rapey'.[169]

The UK charity Stonewall was set up to advance the rights of lesbians, gay men and bisexual people. Nancy Kelly, CEO of the charity, likened lesbians' concerns about the cotton ceiling as being equivalent to 'sexual racism'[170] and also compared so-called 'gender-critical' beliefs to antisemitism,[171] in what some see as an upsetting reversal of Stonewall's original mission. In my opinion, this could also be seen as coercive control, as well as justifying a male expression of power akin to what Wild describes as rape culture.

If the leader of the top lesbian and gay rights charity in the UK has now suggested that the exclusion of males from the concept of lesbianism can be compared to bigotry, this is a clear demonstration of the way in which the conflation of gender-based attraction with sexuality is unhelpful. The belief in gender identity does not benefit lesbians, especially if lesbians are being pressured, whether subtly or overtly, into having sex with males. Lesbianism cannot be reduced to a preference: it must be based on sexuality. Female biology cannot be excluded from that which makes a woman a lesbian, and being male excludes that possibility. The insistence on including males within the definition of lesbianism is also insulting because it denies the difference between the male hetero-/bisexual experience of sexuality and the female experience of lesbian sexuality, and in so doing denies the reality of a minority group. We wind up in practice with a situation in which same-sex attracted women are no longer permitted to have a word which describes this unique experience – as if it isn't distinct from other sexualities.

This chapter contains just a handful of documented examples of discrimination against women and girls, how it has been enabled, sometimes by those seeking to do the right thing, but in all cases where the impact on women was not fully considered or was deemed secondary. Women's spaces and biological

realities are being contested in specialist services for those who
have been subjected to men's violence, in prisons, in coveted
prizes, in sports, in women's toilets, in changing rooms, hospital wards and in the way our bodies are spoken about.

As the trans rights activist movement has progressed, we
have become aware of disturbing examples which illustrate
that the safety and boundaries of women are increasingly
assigned secondary importance to the desires of males who
identify as transgender. Not all males rape, beat, kill, diminish, demean or otherwise harm women. However, the patterns
of victimisation and perpetration are such that women have
developed resources to respond to men's violence against
women. Governments across the world have recognised the
need for such single-sex services by funding and endorsing
them – sometimes in law. 'Not all men are like that' is an
oft-heard lament of those who cannot stop themselves from
prioritising men over women. The cry of 'not all transwomen
are like that' is no different: first, because there is little reliable
evidence to show that self-image and having a trans identity
changes the average male's likelihood of posing danger or
indignity to women; and second, because, as with males who
do not have a trans identity, there is no way of knowing in
advance who has good and who has bad intentions.

What about the men?

Males who identify as transgender, as well as those who do
not, can be victims of domestic and sexual violence and abuse.
This is more likely to be perpetrated by someone of the same
sex in males than it is in females. Males, regardless of whether
they identify as transgender or not if they have been subjected
to sexual or domestic violence and abuse, regardless of the sex
of who perpetrated it, should have access to specialist support
and advocacy services. However, services for males who have

been subjected to sexual and/or domestic violence and abuse should be separate from those for women: first, because males pose a potential risk to women; second, because the presence of males is a barrier to many women's recovery; and third, because men who have been subjected to intimate partner violence and/or including sexual violence, themselves recognise that they have different needs. For example, space to question and challenge gender norms, to reduce their feelings of shame and embarrassment surrounding masculinity and victimisation,[172] though research has found that, of gay men accessing support for same-sex partner abuse, only 43 per cent stated a preference for help from men.[173]

In fact, it is not so unusual for organisations who support women in the community to work with a small number of men, though when they do, it is sometimes because the contract the organisation has with the local authority funding the service requires that support is provided for male victims too, not necessarily because the organisation set out to provide it in the first place. Where males are supported, regardless of their sexuality or gender identity, they should get the same high-quality service and are due the same empathy and respect as women. It is possible to include males with transgender identities in these services and in many cases this already happens, so males with transgender identities are not excluded from all services, just the ones where women victim-survivors are also present. Where an organisation cannot support someone, often they will refer them to an alternative organisation. There are also specialist organisations for men, and also for LGBT+ people.

The possibility of males passing, that is, be read by other people as the sex that they are not, poses challenges to those seeking to provide women-only services, including those for women who have been subjected to men's violence. People who identify as transgender are legally entitled to a strong level of privacy regarding their medical history and status, and, for those who have a GRC, the level of privacy is further enhanced. The sharing of information about a person's transition history, if they have one, is a strict liability criminal offence, which means it is unlawful if someone shares what they have been told in an official capacity. Furthermore, there is no obligation for a trans person to share information if they hold a GRC. So, in the event that someone passes, it is possible that no one would know. In practice, then, I don't think that there is very much that can be done about this. Ideally, those who know they are not female would respect the boundaries of those who are.

6

Sisters are Doing it for Themselves

The fight to preserve single-sex services

Recognising that we are stronger together, a lot of organisations providing support to women victim-survivors of men's violence become members of what are called 'second-tier' organisations, which are supposed to advocate for both the beneficiaries of our organisations (the people who use the services or who share the problems that we're dealing with) and the organisations themselves. A lot of people make the mistake of thinking we're all one large organisation, but we're not, we're all autonomous organisations. The main second-tier organisations in my sector are Women's Aid Federation England (WAFE) for domestic violence and abuse services, Rape Crisis for rape, sexual assault and incest services and Imkaan for specialist services run by and for Black, Asian and women from other minoritised ethnic groups. Until March 2022, when WAFE finally made a clear announcement of their commitment to single-sex spaces,[1] none of the second-tier organisations had spoken out supporting sticking to single-sex services delivery.

It is true that, when their member organisations hold different views (as they do on the inclusion of males who identify as women), second-tier organisations have to hold a space where they can represent all the different perspectives. But they have a responsibility to show leadership and, at the very least, those who pay their annual membership fee should be able to expect clear guidance on the position of the law.

As outlined in chapter 1, the Equality Act identifies a number of areas where it is lawful to exclude one sex, whether or not individuals meet the 'gender reassignment' threshold in the Act (let alone whether they simply declare that they have changed gender).

The very least member organisations could have expected from second-tier organisations was guidance in accordance with the law to make this clear. At the time I wrote nia's policy for prioritising women in our services in 2018, all similar policies already available were explicitly permitted the inclusion of transgender males. I couldn't find a single example of a policy informed by the single-sex exceptions. I have shared nia's policy with several other women's organisations since then and it has been used to inform a model policy on single-sex services by the campaigning group Sex Matters.[2] I am proud that the policy, developed by a small under-resourced charity like nia, taking a risk with the intention of protecting beneficiaries and the legacy of specialist services for women, has had a wider influence. Charities should remain true to their aims (and the law), should prioritise the interests of those they serve and avoid becoming either an arm or a puppet of the state. I will look at how nia decided to speak out later in the chapter.

In an article in *The Sunday Times* in 2018, WAFE was reported as stating, 'We have agreed to start a review of our whole transgender policy, including the possibility of employment for self-declared transgender women without a Gender Recognition Certificate.'[3] The move, not surprisingly, was interpreted as the charity saying that males who self-identified as women would be welcome to work in women's refuges and, by implication, stay in them too.

The next day WAFE responded with a statement, emailed

to members, claiming that the reports, which had appeared in *The Sunday Times*, *Daily Mail*, *Evening Standard*, *The Sun* and *Pink News*, were incorrect and the charity would review its policies and consult with member organisations to assist them in understanding the law and making decisions about services. When the survey to members was circulated roughly a month afterwards, their capture by gender identity ideology was clear to see in the framing of the questions. The survey conflated facts and opinions and used contested terms such as 'gender assigned at birth'. Anyone with an understanding of research and statistics knows about the importance of objectivity and not asking leading questions. The survey had seriously failed this basic requirement.

I wrote to the CEO of WAFE at the time, explaining my concerns. When she didn't reply after two months, I followed up, including the chairs of the board of trustees in my email. This time, I received a reply and was invited to meet one of the co-chairs. It was made clear to me that WAFE had no appetite to fight for single-sex services.

Verdi Wilson worked for Scottish Women's Aid (SWA) until 2021. She raised concerns in a staff group chat that an advertised advisory panel for work with young women had not made explicit that the group was open to males with transgender identities. She was suspended pending investigation as to whether disciplinary procedures would be initiated. After a meeting with her manager, it was decided that the matter would not become a disciplinary issue on this occasion but she was warned against responding to messages in an open team's forum and told that SWA did not expect their policies or practices to be challenged on social media. Verdi felt unable to reconcile her experience-based knowledge that sex is a critical issue regarding men's violence against women with, not only increased acceptance of transgender identity ideology, but also pressure to accept or be seen to accept the same herself, and resigned from her post.

In 2021, I was pleased (and pleasantly surprised) to see WAFE's written submission to the WESC Inquiry on reform of the GRA welcome the government's commitment to retain the single-sex exceptions and defend their protection from accusations of transphobia.[4] This had followed the election of a new board of trustees which increased the representation of those actually running services for women and children on the Board and the appointment of a new Chief Executive, Farah Nazeer. The organisation had finally recognised that shying away from taking a position was not effective and again consulted member organisations promising to take a position after considering their findings. A statement, finally issued in 2022, 12 years after the introduction of the Equality Act, supported those who recognised the importance of women-only services whilst leaving space for those who wished to include those born male in their services for women. Finally, under Nazeer, WAFE asserted that the provision of single-sex domestic abuse services was a founding principle and that they would defend it.[5]

Although the WAFE statement unequivocally committed to supporting the development of specialist services for trans people, SWA and Galop both quickly released statements in response, arguing for support for organisations who included males with transgender identities in their supposed women's services. It was quickly pointed out that SWA had failed to consult member organisations about their position on trans inclusive services and that many did not support it.[6,7]

Also in 2022, the Women's Resource Centre, an organisation which supports the sustainability of women's sector organisations, with a determined focus on marginalised and disadvantaged smaller organisations, also released a statement supporting single-sex services and women's sex-based rights.[8] This was the organisation's first explicit statement, although they had, for years, been releasing research on the importance and value of women's specialist services.[9]

The Fawcett Society

The Fawcett Society describes itself as the UK's leading membership charity campaigning for gender equality and women's rights at work, at home and in public life. Its history can be traced back to 1866, and Millicent Garrett Fawcett's campaigning work for women's suffrage. It became the Fawcett Society in 1953. Despite their proud history, Fawcett's uncritical use of the phrase 'gender equality' and interchangeable use of the words sex and gender are indicative of the charity's current unwillingness to align itself with women's sex-based inequality. It is a tool of patriarchal society serving to enforce and maintain sex inequality. It may be that some women in the organisation share a view similar to my own and may have tried to push the charity into a different position to that which has been publicly expressed, but if this is the case, they have been silenced.

Fawcett's then Chief Executive, Sam Smethers, acknowledged in 2020 that some feminists believe that people are born either female or male, whilst others argue that gender identity is what matters, before going on to say that she would not be limited by either world view. Smethers said that there are some circumstances in which biological sex takes precedence over gender identity, purporting to support single-sex services, and also said that services should meet the needs of 'both groups' and that the answer was not to shut trans people out. Smethers went on to claim that 'transwomen experience the same misogyny in their day-to-day lives as those who are biologically female'. In a seeming attempt to appease everyone, Smethers sat on the fence when, after years of feminists asking for the Society's support, she eventually addressed the threat of transgender identity ideology to women's rights and protections.[10]

Edinburgh Rape Crisis

In May 2021, Mridul Wadhwa, who identifies as a transwoman and reportedly does not have a Gender Recognition Certificate, took up the post as Chief Executive of Edinburgh Rape Crisis. Wadhwa, who by then had worked in three different Scottish sexual and domestic violence victim's support organisations,[11] and was well known in such organisations, had previously not disclosed a biological and legal sex when appointed to one such post, saying 'I wasn't even sure that I would have been hired, had they known that I was trans.'[12] In the announcement of the news by Edinburgh Rape Crisis, Wadhwa said:

> I am especially pleased to be joining the organisation at a time when it is seeking to increase its accessibility to and inclusion of survivors of gender-based violence from marginalised and easy to ignore communities. As a passionate, loud and consistent advocate for the rights of transwomen and Black Minority Ethnic women, I look forward to working alongside my new colleagues to ensure that we provide inclusive and flexible support.[13]

Later, in an interview with Kemah Bob, on the Guilty Feminist podcast, Wadhwa said:

> But I think the other thing is that sexual violence happens to bigoted people as well. And so, you know, it is not discerning crime. . . . But if you bring unacceptable beliefs that are discriminatory in nature, we will begin to work with you on your journey of recovery from trauma. . . . But if you have to reframe your trauma, . . . you also have to rethink your relationship with prejudice.[14]

In making support conditional, Wadhwa is both misunderstanding and setting out an intention to misuse trauma. One of the most basic starting points for those of us working with women, girls and children who have been subjected to men's violence is being woman-centred; you don't help abused women recover self-esteem and self-belief if the first thing you do is tell them that they are bigots. Reframing trauma does not require someone to adopt someone else's belief system. Empowering women is not compatible with compelling them to believe what makes sense to you. That sounds more like a cult or an Orwellian dystopia.

Lest anyone should be tempted to generously give Wadhwa the benefit of the doubt and put the above performance down to unpreparedness, a few weeks later, in an online meeting titled 'Building Intersectional Inclusion in Rape Crisis Services' hosted by the Sheffield-based Sheena Amos Youth Trust (SAYiT), Wadhwa revealed

> You have large groups of survivors, some are not using our services because they see us as trans inclusive and feeling that they may be exposed to . . . er . . . to an issue that they are not prepared to deal with.[15]

In other words, the CEO of Edinburgh Rape Crisis knows that women victim-survivors of incest, rape and sexual assault are not accessing specialist services meant for them because they do not want to be exposed to a male who identifies as a woman. Edinburgh Rape Crisis, like Brighton Survivors Network, has made itself inaccessible to women who are sexual violence survivors experiencing trauma who want to receive support in a woman-only environment.

Bessel van der Kolk, whose influential work on trauma I discussed in chapter 4, addressed shame and low self-worth and how antithetical these were to the recovery process. He said

> Someone who is stern, judgemental, agitated, or harsh is likely to leave you feeling scared, abandoned, and humiliated, and that won't help you resolve your traumatic stress. . . . Traumatised

human beings recover in the context of relationships . . . the
role of the relationship is to provide physical and emotional
safety, including safety from feeling shamed, admonished, or
judged, and to bolster the courage to tolerate, face, and process
the reality of what has happened.[16]

Women accessing Rape Crisis services who are being told that
they are bigots, who are being told that they must accept that
people can change sex or who are not accessing the services
because they either need women-only spaces or refuse to
capitulate to transgender ideology, are being failed.

Even before the appointment at ERC, Wadhwa had given
the impression that the needs of some female victims of rape
were treated as being of secondary importance to the validation of transgender males' identities. In 2020, the Scottish
parliament had voted unanimously in support of the Forensic
Medical Services Bill. The purpose of the Bill was to improve
healthcare services for victims of rape and sexual assault. It
came after it had been revealed that rape victims were having
to wait for up to three days without washing while a female
forensic examiner could be found. The important Bill contained a flaw, however. In a section which was supposed to
give victims choices regarding who carried out a rape examination on them, the word gender had been used instead of
sex. Early concerns about this were rejected, with the Scottish
government denying that there was legislative ambiguity. The
move was supported by Rape Crisis Scotland. Following protests from grassroots feminists, Labour Member of Scottish
Parliament (MSP) Johann Lamont tabled an amendment,
which was referred to as 'six little words' because it said simply
'for the word "gender" substitute "sex"'. Lamont's amendment
embodied the clash between trans rights activism and wom-
en's rights and was certainly viewed in those terms. MSP and
health spokeswoman for Labour Monica Lennon complained
'there are some people who want to exclude transwomen from

working with women and girls to have disclosed rape or sexual assault'. To which Lamont responded: 'Forgive me if I focus on survivors in this debate.' [17]

Johann Lamont's amendment passed with 113 votes for, and nine against (four Liberal Democrats and five Greens). The Scottish parliament demonstrated that they understood that it was important for rape survivors to be able to choose the sex of the person examining them.

Wadhwa accused one MSP of going along with 'those who promote the bigoted contempt for a minority group and have hijacked survivors' trauma to further their cause'. [18] Eight days after the vote, Wadhwa, who had been a member of the SNP and had sought selection as an MSP through an all-women shortlist, had left and joined the Scottish Greens.

It is not just the comments that Wadhwa has made that concern me, but also the message given by appointing a male in a leadership role in what most would perceive as a women's organisation. In fact, the vacancy had been advertised as open only to women. It used to be – and hopefully still is for many – the case that those of us providing services for women from organisations with feminist backgrounds used how we worked to model alternatives to hierarchical structures and sex-role stereotypes. It was a given that women could do anything that men could do. When we used female plumbers, electricians or decorators, for example, it wasn't only to keep males out for safety reasons, though that was part of it, but because we wanted to present positive female role models who defied stereotypes. We should think seriously about which messages about female competency are communicated if the most senior people in an organisation are male, and surely we should take the opportunity to allow women's organisations to lead by example.

There are at least two other organisations, supporting victim-survivors of domestic and sexual violence and abuse – the majority of whom will be female – with male CEOs.[19]

nia – standing alone and standing up for women

In September 2017, I was presenting a draft 5-year strategic plan
to the trustees of nia. Strategic plans outline an organisation's
key priorities and objectives for the coming years. After discussion, they were ready to ratify the plan that I had presented,
but I felt uneasy. We'd looked at threats and opportunities in
the external environment but there was something that we
had not discussed. So, I said that there was one threat we were
facing and that I was concerned that if we did not address it,
we would be complicit in the erasure of single-sex provision.
In the following discussion, we recognised that raising our
voice on this issue was a risk, as the reception to women who
were prepared to challenge the claim that 'transwomen are
women' was even more hostile than it is today. We understood
that there was the potential that reactions could threaten the
survival of the charity. That's not an easy decision to take, as
nia supports up to 2,000 women and girls a year, as well as a
small handful of men, some of whom identify as transgender.[20]
In addition, we provide employment to a number of women.
Nevertheless, the board voted and agreed that if this was the
hill that the charity died on, we would go down proudly fighting for the right to single-sex services for women who had
been subjected to men's violence. The draft strategic plan was
amended and 'protecting women-only services and spaces' was
added to our strategic objectives.

The next job was to produce a policy which outlined how
we would work on a day-to-day basis, delivering the contracts
we held and working within the law. Some of our community-
based services required us to deliver services to men. When
we do this, we do not invite men to places where we deliver
services to women and we do not work with men if we are
supporting their partner. Some organisations had by then
produced 'trans inclusion policies' outlining how they would
include men with transgender identities in their women's

services. It was clear that some people and organisations were – deliberately in some cases, unintentionally in others – promoting a misinterpretation of the Equality Act. It was being claimed that the Equality Act said that organisations could only make decisions about exclusion on a case-by-case basis.[21] We could see that this was not the case, and that it was lawful for organisations to exclude males if it was a proportionate means of achieving a legitimate aim. The Act also requires that those applying single-sex restriction must meet one of six additional conditions which include that a joint service would be less effective, which clearly applied to our services. The Act also permits organisations to employ only women. In 2018, the board of trustees ratified nia's ground-breaking 'Prioritising Women Policy'. We had used the definition of woman as 'adult human female' in the policy before it became the recognisable marketing phrase that it is now.

Grassroots support

As far as I am aware, in 2017, nia was the only UK support and advocacy service for women victim-survivors of men's violence that was taking a public stance in defending the importance of single-sex services for women, girls and children who had been subjected to men's violence. Others were doing so quietly, without announcing what they were doing, and this has continued to be the case. With the exception of nia, those funded to keep women, girls and children safe stayed silent. Aurora New Dawn, based in Portsmouth, declared a similar position to ours in late 2019/early 2020. Apart from these two small charities, the feminist spirit of the earlier movement to support women victims of men's violence seemed to have been extinguished. The silence of those who did not speak out for women left exposed those of us who did so.

Instead, the cry of resistance, galvanised by the government's consultation on proposed changes to simplify the process of gender recognition and their lack of engagement with women, came from grassroots feminists as individuals and also led to the development of new organisations and informal groups who were not prepared to sit back and keep quiet – and which, perhaps critically, had nothing to lose but women's rights. These included an anonymous group of women who were survivors of men's violence, FOVAS (Female-Only, Violence and Abuse Survivors)[22] and Woman's Place UK (WPUK),[23] founded by Kiri Tunks, Judith Green and Ruth Serwotka, which I became part of. The group was formed to ensure that women's voices would be heard in the consultation on proposals to change the Gender Recognition Act. WPUK later formalised its structure and revised its campaigning aims to include a broader approach to women's rights. Other organisations include Fair Play for Women, who amongst other actions, produced a report revealing that women who run and use refuges had grave concerns that legislative changes meant to help transgender people would make it easier for abusive men to enter refuges;[24] Transgender Trend, an organisation of parents, professionals and academics concerned about the diagnosis of children as transgender and providing alternative resources to those produced by groups encouraging gender identity affirmation in young people; Man Friday, a group including Amy Desir and Hannah Clarke who highlighted the absurdity of self-identification by claiming to identify as men on Fridays and invited others to join them taking part in 'random acts of manliness'.[25]

Since then, a number of other groups have emerged, including Get the L Out,[26] Labour Women's Declaration, Keep Prisons Single Sex,[27] Sex Matters[28] and Frontline Feminists Scotland.[29]

Women speaking out for women

Thousands of ordinary women have added their voices, on social and traditional media, in speeches, in meetings, and in action on the streets, making clear that single-sex services matter. It is not possible to cover every single example of women who spoke out for single-sex services but I want to cover some of them here. I apologise to women who I have not been able to include. I know there are many more of us than I can name below and that it is all of us together who are creating change for women and girls who have been subjected to men's violence.

None of the women below are motivated by an anti-trans agenda but rather by the desire to make things better for women who have been subjected to men's violence.

Judith Green was a former service user of Survivors Network in Brighton. She contacted the organisation in October 2017 asking them whether they invoked the single-sex exceptions of the Equality Act or whether their policy had changed. She spoke in a parliamentary seminar, sharing her finding that not a single service for sexual violence survivors in East Sussex was any longer women-only. Nine months after her initial approach to Brighton Survivors Network, her email remained unanswered so she sent a follow-up email. The chair of trustees replied that they used a 'self-identification policy' and as such their services were open to self-identifying women only (in other words, males who identified as women could access). The reply went on to state that this meant that their services continued to be and had always been 'women-only'. They did not acknowledge that they were using a contested definition of 'woman'. If there had been no change to a policy of supporting women only, there was a disingenuous failure to acknowledge that for some, the definition of woman was changing and would now include males.

Children's author Onjali Raúf, who founded Making Herstory following the murder of her aunt by her estranged former husband, spoke about the added pressures on women of some faiths in a Woman's Place meeting. She said: 'Women like myself and my Sikh or Hindu or Jewish friends who need single-sex space places to safely unveil, wash up and reconfigure ourselves; women who have been punched, beaten, raped, and broken at every possible level you can conceive, to be forced to accept former men as part of their healing process, will, to put it bluntly, lead to further trauma, or worse still, a distrust and turning away from the very services they believed might help them.'[30]

Another speaker at a WPUK meeting in 2018, Catia Freitas, spoke about the importance of consciousness raising during her stay in a women's refuge. Catia said 'Alongside safety, time to think and rebuild, I think this was the most important thing the refuge gave me. I cannot imagine how this could be achieved among those for whom womanhood is a look, some clothes, a body to be appreciated in the most diminishing ways a person can be disrespected.'[31]

Joan Smith, author of *Misogynies* and *Home Grown*, was the independent chair of the London Mayor's Violence Against Women and Girls panel from 2013 to 2021. In June 2020, she and I wrote to Sophie Linden, Deputy Mayor for Policing and Crime, raising our concerns about the Mayor, Sadiq Khan, tweeting the manta 'transwomen are women' from his professional Twitter account and the impact that this could have on women, particularly when the Mayor's Office for Policing and Crime (MOPAC) funds so many specialist organisations providing services to women and children subjected to men's violence. He never replied. In 2021, Joan was removed from her unpaid role, by email and with no prior warning in a way that was utterly disrespectful to her years of service. In an article published in 2022, Joan asked 'what happens if the board of a refuge has a different interpretation of the Equality Act from the Mayor? If the CEO refuses access to a male-bodied trans woman . . . will her organisation be . . . accused of transphobia?

Would any service provider funded by the Mayor dare take the risk?'[32]

Finally, JK Rowling has added her voice in solidarity with women, like herself, who have been victims of men's violence. She described her perennial jumpiness, the blind fear of the realisation that the only thing keeping her alive was the 'shaky self-restraint' of her attacker, the memories of a serious sexual assault recurring in a loop in her head. Rowling acknowledged that for some people, especially older people who have the maturity to better comprehend the enormity of the undertaking, transition is a solution and a gateway to a happy life. She ended a deeply personal piece of writing – which was respectful to people with transgender identities throughout, and in which she shared her personal experiences of being abused – with a request for empathy and understanding for the many millions of women who wanted their concerns to be heard.[33] Instead, Rowling has suffered serious harassment including death and rape threats, and threats to be cancelled.[34]

So many women walk through life with the physical, psychological and emotional scars of men's violence. So many women who have been subjected to men's violence will tell you, when asked, that women-only spaces, single-sex spaces, have been critical to their recovery. Others will tell you that they and other women had contentedly shared their recovery space with males who identify as women. I'm glad that they have had positive experiences, but they cannot speak for all women and they cannot erase decades of good practice based on research, experience and women's testimony. Women who are fortunate enough not to need the sanctuary of a woman-only space or service should not take it upon themselves to deny it to those who do.

7

'Trans Rights Are Human Rights'

Claims that the trans rights movement is the twenty-first century's equivalent of the fight for lesbian and gay rights, or for the civil rights movement for racial equality, are drawing upon false equivalences. Lesbians and gay men, Black, Asian or people from other minoritised ethnic groups were not contesting the rights of another marginalised group. The Black civil rights movement was a fight to be seen as of the same value as white people, a fight that can still be witnessed in the Black Lives Matter movement. And there is no criticism implied in saying that transwomen are not women, because in the context of 'misgendering', for example, the person speaking is rarely implying different hierarchical values for females and males. Sociologist Michael Biggs wrote

> There is an affinity between the liberal discourse of human rights and the radical discourse of queer theory: they favour those who are construed as victims of formal institutions of power. The power that can be exercised among individuals, such as that exerted by one inmate over another, is ignored. . . . Thus queer theory recruits the power of the state to buttress its own identitarian logics.[1]

I don't think it's unfair to say that the voices in the trans rights movement almost always prioritise the needs of males and males are the privileged sex in patriarchal society. Meanwhile many of the older lesbians, and indeed heterosexual women and men, as well as gay male allies too who are today accused of transphobia, were involved in campaigns like the protests against Section 28, a dreadful law which prohibited the 'promotion of homosexuality' by local authorities and was introduced by Margaret Thatcher's Conservative government in the late 1980s. It is true that some objectors to the idea that people should be categorised according to gender are motivated by conservative and religious 'anti-progressive' beliefs; transphobia, even, but many of us are not and distance ourselves from socially and politically conservative positions.

The Universal Declaration of Human Rights (UDHR) was adopted by the United Nations General Assembly in Paris in 1948, representing one of the green shoots of hope in the aftermath of the horrors of the Second World War. It recognised all humans as being 'born free and equal in dignity and rights' regardless of 'nationality, place of residence, gender, national or ethnic origin, colour, religion, language, or any other status'.[2] The UDHR enshrines 30 rights and freedoms and includes civil and political rights as well as economic, social and cultural rights, including: rights to life, liberty, privacy, to social security, health, adequate housing, education, asylum, to freedom of expression and, finally, the right to be free from torture.

The UDHR served as a foundation for national and international laws and standards. It was the basis of the European Convention on Human Rights, which was incorporated into UK law by the Human Rights Act (HRA) 1998.

When we say human rights are universal, we mean that they should apply to everyone, irrespective of any other differences between us. 'Trans Rights Are Human Rights' became a prominent slogan of transgender activism and has been widely used on signs and heard in chants outside feminist meetings being held to discuss conflicts arising from the trans debate. I think it's fair to say that the effort to think through these issues in the framework of human rights is both an attempt to lend legitimacy to a campaign that is set on eroding women's sex-based rights, but also an attempt to draw attention to the dehumanisation of transgender people in some arenas.

Some trans rights that are being proposed do come into contradiction with existing women's rights, which many feminists are determined to preserve. The question to ask here is, should these proposed rights – such as self-identification[3] into the legal categories of 'male' and 'female' – be considered fundamental? Is the label of 'human rights' really appropriate here? By labelling the battle as a matter of 'human rights', it is being suggested not only that to deny these requests dehumanises trans people, but that these requests are beyond debate and should be granted immediately with no public discussion on the matter. And some feminists are saying no. No, you cannot remove the rights for which we have fought; no, you cannot deny that there is no conflict; and no, we will not be silenced. As Helen Joyce states

> Having the protected characteristic of gender reassignment does not give someone the right to use facilities intended for the opposite sex: rather, it covers discrimination in work and everyday life, such as being sacked or refused service in a pub.[4]

I've never met a feminist who would seek to deny fundamental rights to those humans who identify as transgender or believe themselves to have some essence of the category that they were not born into. However, males, including those who identify as a woman, transgender or non-binary do not have a fundamental right to enter sports for females. Males, including those who identify as a woman or transgender do not have the fundamental right to compel others to act as if we share their beliefs. Males, including those who identify as a woman or transgender, do not have a fundamental right to enter women's refuges. These are not 'human rights' issues, but the discourse surrounding them often seeks to remove boundaries that are supposed to benefit women, intimating that these boundaries are harmful to trans people. While it cannot be denied that trans rights are in the process of being shaped by public debates, this process is, in my opinion, a necessary one.

I support the concept of universal human rights. I don't think a person who identifies as transgender should face violence or abuse, or discrimination in access to services or employment. I'm a feminist, so it naturally follows that I don't think a person's biology should dictate how they participate in society, what they wear, what qualities their personality should have. We should all be free of socially constructed gendered or sex-role stereotypes. Feminism seeks to free women (and men) from stereotypes, not trap us in them.

All fundamental rights of humans should be respected, but no one else's human rights should diminish those of another person. As I outline throughout this book, women need additional protections in law because society treats us unequally, and in an advanced patriarchal society like the one in which we live, women will never be treated as equal to men. As a result, some legislation needs to operate on the premise of sex. It isn't helpful to deny a clash of interests or not to acknowledge that transgender people's rights should be respected. Recognition of this clash enables us to find solutions that work for everyone. It is clear that trans people, like other minority groups, can face serious challenges to their pursuit of a safe and happy life. Vikki Thompson, who died by suicide in Armley Prison – a male prison – in Leeds had suffered sexual harassment, while 'Mary', a male to transwoman prisoner in Boggo Road Gaol, Brisbane, recounted horrific abuse after being imprisoned for four years after stealing a car, and Jasmine Rose reported suffering multiple rapes and sexual assaults while in prison in America.[5,6,7] A 2018 report on the deaths of 93 women in prisons in England and Wales by the charity Inquest stated that in addition to those deaths, seven transgender women had died in men's prisons since 2007, five of which were self-inflicted.[8] I acknowledge that the right to life and the right to freedom from torture and inhuman and degrading treatment are human rights and these rights should be protected for transgender people just as much as everyone else.[9] More generally, a 2022 report by the London Assembly Health Committee found that transgender people frequently face discrimination, unequal treatment, inappropriate diagnoses and denial of treatment.[10] Meanwhile, in 2020, the Trump administration ruled to remove non-discrimination protections for LGBTQ people in healthcare and health insurance.[11] In Australia, research found widespread reports of healthcare failures in trans-related healthcare.[12] This is not in line with the UDHR's recommendation, which identifies health as part of the right to an adequate standard of living.[13] None of this negates the importance of protecting women's sex-based rights, including access to single-sex spaces, though it is a given that we must not ignore the rights of others and should not ignore the humanity of people with transgender identities. Similarly, transgender people can and have spoken up to support women: for example, a group of transgender activists wrote a public letter to the *Sun* condemning the publication of a story in which JK Rowling's former partner admitted that he had assaulted her and that he was not sorry.[14]

The see-saw of gains and losses in the US, reflecting the transition of power through the Obama, Trump and Biden administrations, shows how quickly women, transgender and anyone from a minoritised background can have precious victories rescinded. In March 2017 Trump revoked the 2014 Fair Pay and Safe Workplaces rule, which included two measures that particularly affected women workers: pay check transparency and the prohibition of forced arbitration clauses for sexual harassment, sexual assault or discrimination claims.[15] In May 2016, Obama had clarified that transgender students were protected from sex discrimination in education programmes and activities, under Title IX. In February 2017, under the Trump administration, the guidance was withdrawn by the US Departments of Justice and Education.[16] The Violence Against Women Act (VAWA), introduced in 1994, was allowed to expire during Trump's presidency during the government shutdown and Republicans blocked immigrant women from being able to access support.[17,18] Trump also opposed a UN resolution to end rape as a weapon of war.[19] However, despite his best efforts, Trump failed to repeal Obama's landmark Affordable Care Act (known as Obamacare).[20] In 2021, Biden reversed Trump's ban on transgender people serving in the military,[21] and reauthorised and strengthened the Violence Against Women Act and issued an Executive Order to improve safety and justice to address the crisis of missing and murdered Indigenous people.[22] Continuing to mark improvements, under Biden, Kamala Harris became the first Black and first Asian-American Vice President and, in 2022, Ketanji Brown Jackson became the first Black woman to sit on the Supreme Court.[23] But nevertheless, documents leaked to Politico showing that the Supreme Court had voted to overturn abortion rights (*Roe v. Wade*) enshrined in a piece of legislation Trump had vowed to overrule, having appointed justices who would vote for exactly that purpose, sadly materialised.[24,25] The takeaway here is, surely, to ask: if the religious Right had not steadily gained in influence, if some feminists had not lent legitimacy to the Right, if some, particularly on the Left, had not lost sight of the importance of biological sex, if the clash between women's and transgender people's rights were faced, wouldn't we have been better fighting together? And, is this a lesson for the future?

The Gender Recognition Act and reform

The UK GRA was passed in 2004, coming into force the following year. It followed a ruling in the European Court of Human

Rights on the case of two males who had transitioned (*Goodwin and I v. the UK Government*), who successfully argued that in failing to recognise their gender identity, the state was violating their human rights, specifically the right to privacy (Article 8 of the HRA) and right to marry (Article 12). The GRA went beyond the requirements of the case, in that acquiring a GRC was not dependent upon surgery. In other words, the GRA served to answer the transgender human rights challenge by creating a legal fiction.

The government announced that the GRA was to be reviewed following recommendations from the WESC, led by Maria Miller MP, in 2016.[26] The WESC had called 20 people (outside MPs) as witnesses to the inquiry which preceded their report. Kathleen Stock summarised those who were called as witnesses thus: eleven of the twenty represented trans activist organisations, while the remaining nine were relatively neutral experts, though some of these were also trans themselves. No women's groups were called to give evidence, though some had made written submissions, and neither was anyone who had voiced concerns about transitioning.[27]

A public consultation on reform of the Gender Recognition Act, which focused on self-identification and simplification/de-medicalisation of the process of changing legally recognised gender followed, running from July to October 2018. This time, grassroots women groups and activists, including Woman's Place UK and Fair Play for Women, ensured that the voices of women were heard. The Government Equalities Office received 102,818 valid responses to the consultation. The report on the consultation was published after much delay in September 2020.[28] Self-identification was not going to be introduced without the impact on women's rights and protections being taken into account.

The responses were published in February 2021. Stonewall had lobbied very effectively, as 39 per cent of the 102,818 valid responses received by the government used an online form hosted by Stonewall. But so too had feminists: an online form hosted by feminist group Level Up accounted for 7 per cent of submissions and one by Fair Play for Women accounted for 18 per cent. Others, including Woman's Place UK had issued guidance and encouraged women to respond individually. Feminist activism had ensured that women's voices were heard.

Shonagh Dillon, whose doctoral research investigated the silencing of feminist discourse on the proposed changes to the GRA, reviewed the submissions and found only six from funded organisations supporting women victim-survivors of men's violence. Three – nia, the Pankhurst Trust and WAFE – expressed support for single-sex services. And three, Rape Crisis Scotland, Suffolk Rape Crisis and Survivors Network (Brighton) advocated for trans inclusion, in other words: mixed-sex services. Dillon concluded:

> If more women spoke up, especially women in privileged positions of power, maybe we would be able to offer some clarity ourselves. I suspect if victims and survivors turn to this blog, they would be entirely justified in feeling exasperated and frustrated with the lack of clarity from the movement, I know I am.[29]

Transgender lobby groups and the single-sex exceptions

The Equality Act and the single-sex exceptions laid out the way for support services for women who have been subjected to men's violence to be single sex. The proposed reforms of the Gender Recognition Act, particularly self-identification, greatly exacerbated the potential for a clash of rights between women. Stonewall, the Scottish Trans Alliance and Gendered Intelligence all used the tactic of piggy-backing unpopular

causes on less contentious ones in order to achieve political
goals (namely sequestering calls for the abolition of the Equality
Act's single-sex exceptions in their responses to the consultation for reform of the GRA), despite later denials of this from
some.

Benjamin Cohen, CEO of Pink News, a 'UK-based online
newspaper marketed to the lesbian, gay, bisexual and transgender community in the UK and worldwide', spoke on Radio
Four's flagship news programme, Today, to discuss Stonewall's
diversity scheme. Presenter Justin Webb asked Cohen about
Stonewall's attempts to abolish legal provisions for single-sex
spaces. After attempting to change the subject, Cohen said
that it wasn't true, that Stonewall had not made attempts to
change the legislation and were merely interested in self-ID.
Cohen went on to claim, 'they aren't campaigning for that,
that's just misinformation being spread by a homophobic
and transphobic media, I'm afraid'. However, it is on record
that Stonewall did advocate for the removal of the protection of women's single-sex spaces, in their submission to the
Women and Equalities Select Committee (WESC) Inquiry on
Transgender Equality submitted on 27 August 2015. Their recommendations included

> A review of the Equality Act 2010 to include 'gender identity'
> rather than 'gender reassignment' as a protected characteristic
> and to remove exemptions, such as access to single-sex spaces.[30]

Stonewall were not the only group using the WESC Inquiry
on Transgender Equality to lobby for the removal of the
Equality Act's single-sex exceptions; Gendered Intelligence's
submission included:

> We need a comprehensive review of the legislation affecting
> trans people (and intersex people) with the aim of deleting the
> exceptions laid out in the GRA 2004 and EA 2010.[31]

The Scottish Trans Alliance's submission included

The Equality Act 2010 should be amended to:

- include gender identity as a protected characteristic
- remove the exception that allows single sex services to discriminate against trans people
- remove the genuine occupational requirement (GOR) allowing some jobs to require applicants must be cisgender and replace it with a GOR allowing posts delivering trans-specific services to require applicants must be transgender.[32]

These three leading trans rights campaign groups are therefore on record as making the removal of single-sex services for women a strategic aim; and the Chief Executive of *Pink News* as denying that this was the case.

Influencing government: through the backdoor silently

It could be argued that trans rights activism has gained advances in policy less by capturing the hearts and minds of ordinary people, not by campaigns aimed at developing understanding and a shared commitment for change, but by tactical subterfuge. To give one example, a report prepared by Dentons,[33] a global law firm, gave advice to trans rights lobbyists on the subject of helping minors to legally change their gender – in other words to obtain paperwork which stated that their sex was not their biological sex – without parental and adult approval. The strategy included advice to 'get ahead of the government agenda', which would give organisations a greater influence on the development of the government's own proposals, to avoid excessive press coverage and exposure and to tie campaigns to more popular reforms.

Another way in which the aims of lobbyists were pursued involved institutional capture. Institutional capture refers to a form of bad practice, which may or may not be intentional, that occurs when an institution, be it a political entity or organisation, begins, knowingly or not, to serve the interest of a particular interest group. In my view the story of the transgender lobby is a story of institutional and policy capture, and the Dentons document suggests that this was recommended as a deliberate strategy.

Another tactic, used in the UK by Stonewall, could be summarised as 'getting points for good practice by demonstrating that you believe transgender identity ideology'. In fact, the selling of gender identity ideology was so successful that the notion of 'going above and beyond the law' took hold as an arbiter of good practice, where inclusion appears to be more important than protecting women's safety, dignity and well-being.

The role of Stonewall in this process has been very lucrative for them, possibly ensuring the charity survived – this in addition to promoting the belief that gender identity is more important than sex in determining the definitions of 'woman' and 'man'. This belief was highlighted in the Employment Tribunal of barrister, Allison Bailey, in May 2022, by Stonewall's Head of Trans Inclusion, Kirrin Medcalf,[34] who said, 'bodies are not inherently male or female'.

When Ruth Hunt became CEO of Stonewall in August 2014,[35] she was heavily lobbied by transgender activists to make the charity trans inclusive. Her first official meeting with trans rights activists took place just over a month after her appointment had been announced.[36] Critically, also the landscape for lesbians and gay men in the UK had changed dramatically since 1990. Significantly, the Marriage (Same Sex Couples) Bill had been introduced into Parliament in January 2013, and on 29 March 2014 the first same sex marriages took place in the UK. It is clear that homophobia has far from been eradicated still today but, arguably, equal marriage represented the last legislative hurdle for lesbian and gay rights. Did Stonewall feel the need to review its mission to remain relevant?

In February 2015, Stonewall announced that it was extending its remit to include the campaign for trans equality alongside lesbian, gay and bisexual equality, and LGB became LGBT. They launched their 'Vision for Change', a five-year plan for trans equality in Britain, in April 2017.[37]

Stonewall had one paid member of staff in 1990. By September 2000, they had 10 members of staff and an income of just under £1 million. By September 2010, their annual income had increased to £2,791,868 and they employed 27 members of staff. By September 2019, their annual income had increased to £7,269,427 by which time they employed 151 members of staff. Their most up-to-date publicly available accounts, covering an 18-month rather than 12-month accounting period ending in March 2021, showed their income to be £11,548,624. This would average out at an annual income of £7,699,082 with a staff team of around 135 people.[38]

Stonewall runs the Diversity Champions programme, which organisations can join to demonstrate good practice in the employment of LGBTQ+ staff.[39] Not long after joining nia as CEO, I looked into registering nia on the programme, naively reasoning that we were a good employer for lesbians, so it should have been something we could have joined. I quickly realised that we couldn't afford it.

Stonewall's accounts, published online at Companies House, also include a breakdown of sources of income. One such source was 'fees'. This is described as follows in the most recent accounts: 'Fee income consists of income from private, public and third sector organisations who join our Diversity Champions workplace inclusion programme or Global Founding Partners Programme, annual contributions from schools or Local Authorities joining our School Champion or education Champions programmes, and charges made for providing Stonewall Speakers for events or related to bespoke consultancy requests'. In the 18 months ending March 2021, Stonewall had brought in £4,920,675 in fees (on average, equivalent to £3,280,450 in one year). In the year ending September 2019, the equivalent income was similar: £3,269,477. This means that approximately 43 per cent of Stonewall's income derives from charges it makes for its Diversity Champions scheme and similar activities. A further income of £536,900 was raised in the same period from activity related to attending any of Stonewall's empowerment programmes, such as LGBT leadership and the Trans Ally programme).[40]

Stonewall makes over £3 million a year from, it reports, around 900 organisations, keen to demonstrate how inclusive they are. This would be admirable, except for one thing: inclusion is dependent on demonstration of adherence to the current trans rights orthodoxy, with no room for dissent, however reasonable. Until recently, paid-up organisations to the Diversity Champions scheme included the Home Office, the House of Commons, the House of Lords, the Treasury, the Green Party, the Labour Party, the BBC, Channel 4, Citizen's Advice, 95 local authorities, 94 NHS and healthcare bodies, 121 universities and 81 law firms.

Of 34 non-governmental organisations (NGOs, independent charities, etc.), I could only see one Stonewall Champion with female beneficiaries: Girlguiding. This perhaps shines a light on Girlguiding opening their membership to all those who identify as girls or women.

Several children/youth NGOs (in addition to Girlguiding) are signed up to the Diversity Champions scheme, including Action for Children, Barnardo's, Save the Children, the Youth Sport Trust, Princes Trust and Teach First.[41] In addition, bearing in mind what I looked at in chapter 3 regarding the dependence of specialist organisations supporting women victims-survivors of men's violence on local authority funding, it is apparent how the influence of the Diversity Champions scheme stretches beyond those actively signed up to it, as the local authorities (95 of which signed up to the Diversity Champions scheme) are encouraged to require or promote the Stonewall endorsed values in their contracting with third parties, including groups they fund to provide services to women who have been subjected to violence and abuse by men.

The list of Stonewall's Diversity Champions is what influence and institutional capture look like – and institutions such as those listed above have been happy to pay for the privilege. However, it is possible that Stonewall's lobbying techniques and their approach to pushing an inflexible transgender agenda, irrespective of the impact on women's sex-based rights and protections, has led to an increasing number of organisations abandoning the scheme. The campaign group Sex Matters has been tracking organisations leaving the Diversity Champions programme and has, to date, identified over 80 organisations, including the BBC, the Ministry of Justice, Ofsted, Crown Prosecution Service and the Government Equalities Office. It will be interesting to see how this affects Stonewall's fee-generated income and whether in time, this will affect their cavalier attitude to women's rights, including of course lesbians, who are supposed to be one of the groups they represent.[42]

On International Transgender Day of Remembrance (TDOR) in November 2020, Sussex Police raised a 'transgender pride' flag and Hertfordshire Police released a video pledging to fight trans hate crime. In London, the Bank of England was lit up in the pink and blue colours of the trans flag.[43] Five days later, on the International Day for the Elimination of Violence Against Women (IDEVAW, 25 November) in an open letter published in *The Independent*, celebrities including Olivia Colman, Jameela Jamil and Paloma Faith and MPs including Nadia Whittome and Zarah Sultana, condemned 'violence and hostility' against transgender people and repeated the unsubstantiated claim that 'trans women are more likely to be murdered'.[44] Despite TDOR falling a mere five days before, the IDEVAW was chosen as the day to release this letter, which

also said 'To our trans sisters on this day: we are with you.' The
letter did not address women victims of men's fatal violence.
There is no international day to commemorate women killed
by men. Referring to the police action to mark TDOR, retired
Detective Superintendent Caroline Goode commented, 'I have
not personally seen a single police force show any publicity or
any support for the international day for the elimination of violence against women. Every woman's life is absolutely precious,
but you don't see that same sense of outrage in the public arena
at women being murdered as maybe with some other groups.'[45]
Neither was the Bank of England lit up to mark the occasion.

Research

The cloak of notionally objective research to present a sub-
jective perspective is another tactic that has been used by
Stonewall.

Shonagh Dillon, who is also the Chief Executive of Aurora
New Dawn, a registered charity giving safety, support, advocacy and empowerment to survivors of domestic abuse, sexual
violence and stalking, introduced me to the concept of 'claimsmaking'[46] as a strategy for influencing policy. She explained
that claimsmakers use impassioned arguments which can be
based on false narratives and which can disregard, misinterpret
or twist statistical evidence to suit their agenda. Claimsmakers
seek to appeal to the emotions of their audience, including
the press, the public and policy-makers. According to Dillon,
'claimsmakers represent the loudest voices and achieve the
biggest gains in relation to policy influence'.[47] For her doctoral
thesis, she analysed a piece of research by Stonewall purporting to address the views of professionals delivering support
in domestic and sexual violence services which claimed that
those professionals believed that supporting male clients with
a transgender identity would have no negative impact on

female victim survivors. Dillon observed that Stonewall had a unique and significant impact on the debate about access to services for women who have been subjected to men's violence. According to Dillon, Stonewall 'put themselves in a unique position of claimsmaking through their own research interviewing 15 professionals from 12 national umbrella bodies and frontline services in the men's violence against women sector: reporting gender reform would have no impact'. However, she continues, 'when I spoke to a third of their participants, the answers they gave me were far more nuanced and did not support mixed-sex provision'.[48]

Dillon's explanation of claimsmaking and the way that such claims then affect policy can be illustrated by this example from a sitting of the Women and Equalities Select Committee looking at reform of the GRA in parliament in 2021. Angela Crawley MP[49] asked a question of attendees about the levels of male violence towards a hypothetical person she described as a 'trans female [who] has transitioned'. She repeated the claim that in comparison to females such a person is at 'perhaps greater risk of the same violence and the same issues that you've expressed around patriarchy'. This claim, made by a British MP, working in a body which is supposed to hold the government to account on equality law and policy, including the Equality Act 2010 and cross government activity on equalities, is false. At the point that Crawley came out with the claim, it had been over two years since the last murder of a trans person in the UK (Amy Griffiths in January 2019).[50] As far as I am aware, no individual who was publicly known to identify as trans has yet been murdered in Scotland and no female who has transitioned has yet been identified as a murder victim in the whole of the UK. However, between the murder of Griffiths and Crawley's question in Parliament, at least 17 women had been killed by men in Scotland. It does not follow that pointing out that Crawley made a false claim means that I do not believe that trans people are subjected to violence and/or discrimination – sometimes because they are trans. Nonetheless, Crawley's intentions may have been laudable – seeking to ensure that transgender people have access to support – but she has fallen victim to claimsmaking. She is repeating and reinforcing these claims, rather than being led by accurate data and doing so in a government body that is supposed to address women's inequality. I have shown in chapters 4 and 6, it is women who lose out when single-sex services for women who have been subjected to men's violence cease to operate as such.

In addition to the Stonewall report claiming a lack of need or support for single-sex services, research on suicide and trans people, homicides of trans people and hate crimes against trans people has been used to push the gender identity agenda, whilst research challenging the orthodoxy has been blocked.

Suicide research

Declarations about how mixed-sex services have been embraced by specialist providers are not the only examples of overreach in the attempt to create urgency around the issue of responding to the needs of people with transgender identities.

Stonewall[51] and Mermaids[52] (the latter describing itself as helping gender-diverse kids, young people and their families) both have data accessible via their websites about the alarming rates of suicide attempts by young trans people. The issue was picked up by *The Guardian* in 2014, which ran an article by Patrick Strudwick, alleging that '48% of trans people under 26 said they had attempted suicide, and 30% said they had done so in the past year, while 59% said they had at least considered doing so.'[53] Mermaids made the claim that suicide and self-harm were serious risks in a submission to the WESC inquiry into the need for GRA reform and the claim was also repeated in the WESC report.[54] As I noted in chapter 2, Transgender

Trend and Fair Play for Women have looked into the research used to support the claims made by Stonewall and Mermaids. The statistics come from three main sources, two in the UK and one in the US:

- The LGBT charity PACE released a report in 2015 on research which, amongst other things, asked people who chose to, to answer a questionnaire about their history of considering and attempting suicide. A total of 2,078 responses were analysed, of which 120 were from people who self-identified as transgender and of those, 27 were aged 26 or less. Of those 27 young people aged under 27 who identified as transgender, 13 said they had attempted to take their own life in the past. It is highly irresponsible – as well as just poor research practice – to generalise claims from such a small sample of people, especially when they are self-selected and when there are no controls on other variables (in other words, they did not look to see whether anything else might be responsible for the rate of suicide attempts, like homophobic bullying from peers, lack of acceptance from parents, histories of abuse and so on).[55]

- Stonewall commissioned research looking at young people aged between 11 and 19 who identified as lesbian, gay, bisexual or transgender. Again, a selection of children or young people were told about the research and chose whether or not to fill in a questionnaire. This is called non-probability sampling and means that the research tends to look at those who are interested in the subject matter in the first place. This time, 3,717 responses were analysed. They found extremely high levels of self-harm (84 per cent), even higher levels of suicidal thoughts than the PACE study (92 per cent) and a similar level of suicide attempts (48 per cent). Although this time the sample was larger, there are similar problems to the PACE research: a self-selected sample, a lack of control for other things that might have made a difference and no comparison figure for a broader group of children who did not identify as LGBT.[56]

- The third study comes from research in the US. This looked at a much bigger sample, 121,000 young people aged 11–19. This research found that the group most likely to say that they had tried to end their life were gender-non-conforming young women, regardless of either whether or not they identified as transgender, or their sexuality.[57]

In research, it is acceptable to have biased samples if you are looking at a particular issue or a particular group of people, but you cannot simply extrapolate findings from those people to the wider population unless you can demonstrate that you have rigorously controlled the sample of people that you have looked at and qualify your claims. It's like saying 50 per cent of people who were run over by a bus had had a shower that morning and then saying that 50 per cent of people who have showers in the morning will be run over by a bus. Statistics don't work like that. Even if they do not make these claims, this doesn't stop them being manipulated as propaganda, for example by people who for whatever reason don't want to have a shower in the morning or, more pertinently, perhaps, people who want to overstate the grave dangers of showering.

The first two studies did not reveal the sex of the young people who reported attempts at, or thoughts about, taking their lives. They could also have mainly been young women, young women struggling with not lack of gender transition but the transition to their adult women's bodies, with sexualisation and the many other confines of sexist limitations and conditions facing young women as they become adults. Such details are important. Michael Biggs states that 'It is irresponsible to exaggerate the prevalence of suicide. Aside from anything else, this trope might exacerbate the vulnerability of transgender adolescents.[58] There is also contradictory evidence about whether transition had a long-term impact, good or bad. In fact, one study found that people who had transitioned medically had higher rates of suicide attempts than those who had not.[59]

Claims about high rates of self-harm, suicidal thoughts and suicide attempts are not only a serious issue for policy-makers and those drafting legislation: they are also a grave concern for caregivers and parents of children and young people who are struggling with the impacts of puberty and how socially constructed gender stereotypes are enforced according to sex. It is unethical to use people's rightful concerns to push an ideological agenda based on misleading statistics, to state or imply that not affirming gender dysphoria could lead to a young person killing themselves.[60] In fact, the Samaritans, who support people in mental health crisis, caution against speculation about the trigger or cause of suicide, warn that young people in particular are susceptible to suicide contagion, and recommend that coverage of suicide should include that it is preventable.[61] Sadly, this, however, has not stopped the Samaritans themselves from using statistics like the ones above about the links between transgender identities and suicide rates.[62]

Homicide statistics

We don't know how many people in the world have transgender identities, but estimates based on data collected from 27 countries suggest that 2 per cent of people worldwide identify as transgender, gender fluid or non-binary.[63] Two percent of the global population is in the region of 159,603,562 people. Research in the US estimated that, in 2016, 0.56 per cent identified as transgender but that this was increasing and had doubled since their earlier estimate in 2011.[64] Transgender Europe (who use the acronym TGEU) recorded the deaths of 375 trans and gender-diverse people worldwide between

1 October 2020 and 30 September 2021, the majority of the murders being committed in Central and South America (70 per cent), with homicides in Brazil alone accounting for 33 per cent of global deaths.[65]

Casting aside the concern that the two sources above are using two different definitions for the people that they're referring to, this would mean that one trans or gender-diverse person was killed for every 319,207 transgender, gender fluid or non-binary people. We don't know how accurate the estimation of the percentage of transgender, gender fluid or non-binary is, but if we gave them a margin of error of 1 percent either way, it would mean that one transgender person was killed per year for every 212,805 (1 percent of the world's people) to 425,609 (3 percent of the world's people) trans people. Meanwhile, we know that an estimated 87,000[66] women are killed each year out of a global population of just under four billion women (estimated 3,953,737,839), or one woman for every 45,445 people. In other words, depending on how big we assume the world population of transgender people to be, the number of women killed as a proportion of women in the world is between 4.7 and 14 times bigger than the number of trans people killed as a proportion of the number of transgender people in the world.[67] In other words, women are at between 4.7 and 14 per cent greater risk of homicide than trans people. And if we adjusted our calculation based on the estimation that 26 per cent of the world's population is aged 15 or under,[68] then the number of women for every femicide decreases to one femicide per 33,629 women and women would be at between 6.3 and 19 per cent greater risk of homicide than trans people.

STILLTish, a woman who uses this pseudonym to protect her family's identity, looked at global reports of the murders between 2010 and 2020 of 350 people who identified as transgender.[69] Analysing the data, she found that 98 per cent of those killed globally were male. 79 per cent of those killed in the US were Black or from another minoritised ethnic group.

In Europe, 50 per cent of the people killed were immigrants, 62 per cent of whom were involved in the sex trade – a notoriously dangerous form of exploitation.

There are significant differences in homicide and femicide rates and circumstances globally, and just as we cannot base UK policy on murder in general on data from other places, neither can we draw concussions or develop policy on the murders of people with transgender identities in the UK on what is happening in other parts of the world. People presenting in ways not stereotypically associated with their sex does not give anyone an excuse to kill them, and neither, of course, does a person's ethnicity, legal citizenship status or the fact that they have been exploited in the sex industry. But we cannot say that these people were killed because they were transgender or because of transphobia. A conclusion that we can legitimately draw is that if we are comparing the murders of people who identify as transgender to people who do not, in order to determine whether trans people are uniquely vulnerable in this respect, we would need a very specific control group for any comparison to be meaningful. For example, if we compared the deaths at work of people who ate a bar of chocolate every day (and happened to be construction workers),[70] people who ate an apple a day (and happened to be estate agents) and people who ate a baked potato every day (and happened to be nuns), we could not claim that data on the number of fatalities at work experienced by those people was as a result of their dietary habits. If there was a pattern between eating habits and accidents at work, it would be called a spurious correlation, in other words, something else would be behind the association. When we are looking at statistics about groups of people and what happens to them, we have to compare like for like (have a controlled sample) and we have to be able to distinguish between causal and spurious correlations. People from minoritised racial and ethnic groups, people with insecure immigration and people exploited in the sex industry are already at a higher risk of homicide; we cannot deduce that a transgender identification puts them at higher risk but we can be sure that racism and commercial sexual exploitation does, because we have the data.

Back to the UK: there are records of eight males with transgender identities killed in the UK since 2009, plus one gay man who reportedly occasionally 'cross dressed', although there is no suggestion that he identified as transgender in any reports I've seen.

A country's homicide rate is presented as deaths per 100,000 individuals per year. The UK adult female population is approximately 33,940,000 and for males it is 33,150,000. Given Stonewall include non-binary people in their estimation, let's assume the upper government estimate of 50,000 trans people (especially since that estimate dates from 2018). I've already mentioned that more than twice as many men are killed than women every year and that they're most often killed by other men. The UK homicide rate for women is 0.48 (that is, on average, annually 0.48 women are victims of homicide per 100,000 women, or almost one woman is killed a year for every 200,000 women in the population). For men, the rate is 1.14 and for the estimated number of trans people, it is 1.45, so much closer to that for men than that for women.

I have also looked at the number of killings committed by women, men and people who identify as transgender compared with the number of victims of homicides. According to ONS data again, there were 406 women and 4,538 men convicted of homicide in England and Wales in the 11 years ending March 2020. Compared with the number of homicide victims, this shows that 8 per cent more men are convicted of homicide than are victims, and there are 78 per cent fewer females who are convicted of homicide than those who are victims. I found reports of thirteen homicides committed by male individuals who would fall within Stonewall's umbrella term 'trans' during the same time period (remember, there were eight victims, all biologically male), so there were 38 per cent more trans perpetrators than there were victims. Hence, we see a pattern that is neither the same as that for females or males, but much closer to that for males than females.

I've been challenged several times by people insisting that most of the thirteen killers were not 'really' transgender and that we can't know how many of them would self-identify as such. But I've never been challenged about the eight victims in the same way; on the contrary, any challenges have been to inform me that that number is likely to be an undercount because other people who identify as transgender could have been killed and we don't know about their identity. It has to work both ways, however, and I've applied the same investigative criteria to both perpetrators and victims.

There's another similarity with male homicides too. Keep in mind that I said that 49 per cent of all known female homicide victims were killed by a current or former partner, and amongst men it was 3.3 per cent. Of the eight (male) trans people killed between 2009 and 2019, only one was killed by a current or former partner (12.55). Again, then, a pattern much closer to that of males than females emerges.

Of course, these figures do not meet the standards of academic rigour: I've already said that we don't know how many people with transgender identities there are and I'm relying on media reports to identify transgender victims and perpetrators, so it's more than possible that I could be missing people from either category. But this is true of other male and female murder victims too; consider the fact that there's an increasing body of evidence about murders being disguised as overdoses, other accidents or suicides, and none of Shipman's murders were considered as such for a very long time, so in all cases a margin of error needs to be brought into the figures.

I want to make clear that I think every one of those people's deaths is a tragedy. Each of these lives taken is appalling and leaves long legacies of pain for those who loved the victim.

But I want to stress that my work is motivated by prioritising women, especially women, girls and children who have been subjected to men's violence. I think killing people because they do not conform to the gendered expectations associated with their sex abhorrent. Nevertheless, it is our duty as engaged citizens and researchers to draw legitimate conclusions from the data presented to us, and from this we cannot deny that women are at greater risk. Since the last known murder of a transgender person in the UK (in January 2019), at least 430 women have been killed by men.[71]

Crime data

Another important area where the emphasis on the importance of gender identity over sex and men's violence against women intersect is the recording of crime data. In 2019, Fair Play for Women made 51 Freedom of Information requests (to 46 regional police forces, and the Transport Police, Civil Nuclear Constabulary, Ministry of Defence Police, National Police Air Service and the Port of Dover Police) in order to find out how the police record the sex of a suspect when a crime is reported. Twenty of the 51 did not respond. Of the 31 that did, 16 police forces, so almost half, said they recorded data under self-declared gender rather than sex.[72] This would include violent and sexual crimes and could have a serious impact on sex crimes in particular, where female rates of perpetration are low. Crime statistics are used to develop policy and legislation. We do not need policy to be developed on the basis of a false picture of an increase in female-perpetrated violence and sexual crime. If the perpetration of crimes of intimate partner, and sexual violence (though these are by no means mutually exclusive) show diminishing sex differences, it could be misused to argue that evidence supports a declining need for women-only support or an increase in the need for provision for male victims, at the expense of that for women. In 2020 Fair Play for Women, led and won a legal challenge to the Office for National Statistics which would require people to record their legal sex not gender identity in the Census.[73] Subsequently, the Home Office asked police forces in England and Wales to identify transgender victims and perpetrators of crime by their birth sex to bring police data in line with census data. As a spokeswoman for Fair Play commented 'This is a direct result of our win in the High Court last year . . . [it] means that male rapists will no longer be recorded as female in police crime stats.'[74] However, concerningly, trans activists claimed that this would discourage trans victims of crime from reporting crime as they would fear being misgendered.[75]

8

Despatches from 'Terf Island'

Feminist history is a history of battling the straitjacket of gender and men's attempts to define and constrain women. In this concluding chapter I will look at feminist resistance to gender identity ideology in the UK and how this offers hope, but also voice some points of caution about how we must not lose sight of the wider goals of feminism. The word TERF, which stands for 'trans-exclusionary radical feminist', is thought to have entered the lexicon in 2008. I think those influenced by radical feminism recognised the threat of transgender rights activism to women's rights before many others, but today that awareness is more widespread and 'TERF', like the accusation of transphobia, can be used by trans activists to denote anyone posing the mildest challenge to the legitimacy of gender identity ideology. Though there are many ways of defining and differentiating radical feminism from other forms of feminism, the fundamental characteristic is that nothing less than the complete overturn of patriarchal institutions and culture will liberate women and that compromise is collusion that will only serve to mire us within the confines of patriarchy. Radical feminists recognise the role of men's violence against women as a public and private form of control of women.

The UK has earned the nickname 'Terf Island' because of the successes of groups resisting the lobbying for trans rights at the expense of women's rights. Women's grassroots groups, like WPUK and others, worked to make sure that backdoor lobbying was disrupted, agendas were exposed and women's voices were heard. The struggles of women are not a single-issue matter. Women do not lead single-issue lives, and for the majority of women, the inequalities intersecting their lives are multiple. Neither do we need to deny the rights of others to prioritise the rights of women. We do not need to deny that males can be victims of abuse. We do not need to deny males and people with transgender identities the right to develop specialist services in order to assert the boundaries of our own. Putting women first is not hate.

Many today described as TERFs would not describe themselves as radical feminists. Some – like me – might instead be more inclined to describe ourselves as socialist feminists. And anyway, no one is *excluding* trans people from anything for being trans, even if some have philosophical concerns about the way gender is being legitimised today. We are instead saying that sex is immutable and a relevant consideration in a vast array of contexts, and that it is socially constructed gender and structural inequality that must change. We will fight for recognition of our right to exclude males from women-only spaces and to retain the legislative tools to fight sexism, misogyny and men's innumerable violations of women.

Though many still maintain that 'TERF is a slur', it is hard for those who have more recently entered the arena of the feminist struggle, or even the resistance to transgender identity ideology, to know what a powerful silencing tool it was a decade or more ago. In fact, what is tolerated now was a lot harder to say even four or five years ago. I no longer care if someone calls me a TERF; the word has lost that power for me. Some women, and some men, describe themselves as gender-critical. That's not a description I use for myself. I'm a feminist and of course feminism requires an understanding of the system of gender; it would be almost meaningless without it, but without the broader framework of feminism, the concept of 'gender criticism' is poorer.

The largest ever study of government responses to violence against women and girls looked at 70 countries from 1975 to 2005 and found that the most important factor influencing policy change was feminist activism. It played a more critical role than either left-wing governments, the number of women in power or national wealth.[1] Women, feminists, have always spearheaded support and reform for women facing men's violence. This book is my plea for us to protect the precious legacy of our fore-sisters and, quite simply, to put women, girls and children who have been subjected to men's violence first.

Despite being let down by mainstream politics and many whom we would expect to have spoken up for women who have been subjected to men's violence, grassroots feminism has created space for optimism. I have focused on the UK in this book but the push back against women's single-sex spaces by trans rights activism is happening across the globe, as is the feminist fightback. 'Terf Island' offers a beacon of hope to women in many other countries, though we can also see resistance building momentum and achieving gains outside the UK. In June 2022, FINA, the international federation recognised by the International Olympic Committee (IOC) for administering international competitions in aquatics, released a new policy which will require that male transgender competitors and those with 46 XY DSD competing in women's sports have 'not experienced any part of male puberty beyond Tanner Stage 2 or before age 12, whichever is later'.[2] In effect, this will bar males with DSDs and transgender males from competing in elite women's swimming competitions. FINA also said that they would develop an 'open' category, which, said president, Husain Al-Musallam, 'will mean that everybody has the opportunity to compete at an elite level'.[3]

There are a wide range of background perspectives amongst the growing number of people who are concerned about the growth in influence of transgender ideology, and also a range of primary concerns. Some, like me, are particularly interested in women who have been subjected to men's violence. Others may have come to the issue through child safeguarding and development concerns, especially with regard to the rapidly growing number of young people, mainly girls, who act upon the idea of transitioning or of avoiding womanhood and embark on irreversible hormonal and surgical treatment that some subsequently regret. Some concerns include free speech in education, academia and beyond. Others have come across the impact of trans rights activism on women through sports, employment, reproductive rights, women's representation or other issues regarding women's sex-based rights and protections, including our right as women to identify ourselves as a sex class. Women and men entering into this issue are almost always doing so from the position of advocating for women and upholding our ability to name reality – not because they are hostile to trans people, not because they are transphobic, and holding neither an extreme or irrational aversion to non-conformism.

Young women account for a significant proportion of the rapidly increasing groups of people who take on transgender identities. They are now increasingly visible in the detransitioning movement. Many have been left infertile through surgery or puberty-blocking hormones, will have lower voices and masculine facial hair for the rest of their lives, many have undergone double mastectomies of healthy breasts, some while they were still teenagers. The case of Keira Bell is a story of an unhappy young woman with a difficult home life, struggling with becoming an adult. At 14 Keira had begun to feel uncomfortable with her body and the idea of becoming a woman. Three one-hour appointments later she was on puberty blockers at age 16, cross-sex hormones at 17 and by the age of 20 she had had a double mastectomy. Within a couple of years, however, she was facing profound regret and by the age of 23 she was pursuing a legal challenge against the Tavistock and Portman NHS Trust alongside a woman called Mrs A, who is the mother of a then 15-year-old autistic girl who was also on the pathway to transition.

Keira's argument was that children cannot properly consent to taking hormone drugs. In December 2020, the high court deemed that it was 'highly unlikely' that a child under 13 would be able to consent to the treatment, further that it was 'doubtful' that a child of 14 or 15 would understand the consequences. However, appeal judges decided that doctors should use their clinical judgement rather than it being necessary to obtain a court's approval to provide treatment, which overruled the previous High Court judgment.

Keira Bell, who now recognises that the promised goal of becoming a man was never in reality a possibility, said (at the time of writing) that her next steps will be seeking permission to take her case to the Supreme Court.

> The consequences of what happened to me have been profound: possible infertility, loss of my breasts and inability to breastfeed, atrophied genitals, a permanently changed voice, facial hair. I do not want any other young person who is distressed, confused, and lonely as I was to be driven to conclude transition is the only possible answer. I was an unhappy girl who needed help. Instead, I was treated like an experiment.[4]

Keira has played a unique part in the resistance to rapid access to affirmative treatments for young people. Her case illustrates the problem of the affirmative approach, when therapists, teachers, parents and those with positions of influence over a child, or even an adult, endorse the idea of the possibility of changing sex, as in Keira's case; or as may currently be more likely, of the existence of an innate 'gender identity'. The affirmative approach encourages children and young people who are experiencing problems reconciling their future with society's restrictive gender roles, to follow their ideas about transitioning and change their bodies, rather than change society.

One of the critical schisms that exists between those who recognise that transgender identity ideology is a threat to women's rights concerns the recognition of single-issue campaigns and political allegiances between those who share a common concern about transgender identity ideology but little else politically beyond that. Women's right to organise as a sex class and fight for liberation from subjugation and male domination in a patriarchal society, created by men and serving men's interests, is a feminist issue, but knowing that there are two sexes and that people cannot change sex need not be. I believe that forging links with those with whom we would not otherwise politically associate is treacherous and ultimately damaging. Others disagree, claiming that transgender identity ideology is the biggest single threat to women's rights and all else is secondary.

Women do not lead single-issue lives. To me, claiming to care about women's rights is antithetical to not caring about inequalities between women. Feminism cannot ignore racism, social and economic class inequality, lesbophobia or unequal rights of disabled women. With the notable exceptions of some individual MPs, all the mainstream political parties fell to their knees to embrace transgender identity ideology and abandon any pretext of seriously tackling sex inequality, though some senior Conservatives, including the then Prime Minister Boris Johnson, appear to be breaking free of the tyranny of group-think.[5] If, for a moment we accept that it is gender identity that is important and not sex, how would we be able to continue to quantify indicators of sex inequality. Labour, the Greens, the Lib Dems, Scottish Nationalists and the Conservatives have all willingly (it would appear) jumped feet first into the rabbit hole, or refuse to enter the debate, and in doing so leave the assault on women's rights unchecked. Refusal to engage is refusal to protect. Although Liz Truss, in her capacity as Minister for Women and Equalities, eventually pledged to protect single-sex spaces in 2020, it was Maria Miller, formerly in the same role, who had announced the aim of reviewing the GRA and the introduction of self-identification, with scant, if any regard for the impact on women's rights. I was surprised to hear Miller claim, in the House of Commons during the International Women's Day debate in March 2022, that risk assessments were being used to ensure that spaces are kept safe whether people are men, women or trans (it's splitting hairs, perhaps, to point out that trans people are not a separate group). But I had given evidence at a meeting of the Women and Equalities Select Committee chaired by Miller herself which confirmed that precisely what Miller claimed to be the case was not and was not even possible in reality.

I also do not accept that what looks like shared goals on the surface should lead to collaboration without question. Cross-party alliances on some issues, like men's violence against women, can be very effective. But cross-party alliances, such as between Labour, the Scottish Nationalists and the Conservatives, are not the same as working with the far right. Allegiances with the far or religious right are as counterproductive as they are incompatible with the goals of feminism. The religious right has more influence in the US than in the UK, though some UK women have sought links. Jayne Egerton wrote about this in a piece in the feminist journal, *The Radical Notion*.[6] She explored the role of the religious right in the election of Donald Trump and some of the key organisations connected through the interfaces of the American religious right and feminist organisations. The rise of the religious right has its roots firmly in patriarchy and male power and it grows amongst the weeds of other forms of religious fundamentalism, an attempt by those who historically held power to resist

non-conformism. Just as Dentons suggested to Stonewall and
other transactivist organisations the political strategy of hiding
unpopular political goals behind those with mass appeal, the
demand for women to be recognised as a sex class and the
existing provisions in law that are supposed to address sex
inequality and the threat of men's violence and abuse, cannot
be used as a lever for the roll back of rights around women's
bodily autonomy or lesbian and gay rights. Ultra-conservative
notions of the sanctity of the family and standing with those
who can identify sex oppression and the systematic abuse of
women in 'other' cultures, but not its same systemic power
in their own, do women no favours and share the tarnish of
fundamentalism.

The problem of the rising right, however, is not restricted
to the US – though it is arguably less embedded in religious
conservatism, racism is no less a core tenet. In Europe, far right
populist parties are increasingly using women's rights rhetoric
to attract female support, including, for example, the Brothers
of Italy, Alternative für Deutschland (Germany), the National
Rally (formerly Front National) (France), Danish People's
Party and the Progress Party (Norway).[7] Marine Le Pen, president of the National Rally in France, said 'I am scared that the
migrant crisis signals the beginning of the end of women's
rights.'[8] Similarly, in the UK, UKIP was accused of using
'women's rights as a trojan horse to attack minorities'.[9] Those
claiming to defend women's rights whilst aligning with white
supremacists, sometimes in the name of 'increasing reach',
have opened the rest of us, who loathe the politics of their
metaphoric bedfellows, up to such labels as 'white feminism',
'carceral feminism', 'old woman feminism', even 'fascists';[10]
and this could understandably deter potential defenders of
women's rights with progressive goals: 'It's a grim irony that,
by insisting on a "feminism" without any trans women in it,
TERFs have wound up constructing the tool by which fascists aim to destroy feminism altogether', writes Jude Doyle.[11]

Though my own analysis of the cause is different, in that I see the issue of allegiances with the far right as the problem, not defence of women's sex-based rights and protections, I share the fear of the possible outcome.

Similarly, mixed-sex public spaces might exclude women from conservative religious groups, for example facilities such as single-sex swimming sessions, and this is a reason for supporting such provision. At the same time, we must resist attempts to exclude women or segregate them in public spaces as advocated from religious fundamentalist positions. Yasmin Alibhai-Brown was one of a number of feminist anti-fundamentalists who decried the Islamic Education Research Academy's (IERA) attempts to impose sex segregation in lectures at British universities. Saleem Chagtai of IERA argued that they should be permitted on the basis of 'tradition, culture or religion'.[12] For Alibhai-Brown, such practices 'endorse the most offensive prejudices about women: that they are a social and moral peril and if they sit with men, pornographic fantasies or molestations will make it impossible for anyone to concentrate on lectures'.[13] One of the critical questions is whether or not the single-sex space supports the participation of or discriminates against the oppressed group in public life or spaces.

Quite simply, I do not think that feminists should work in cooperation with right-wing traditionalists of any ilk, neither should we look the other way when others do; yet we cannot allow ourselves to be silenced as a result. Being female never intersects with being male but feminism is demeaned if it does not address the intersection of sex with other oppressions.

In the lead-up to the election of Keir Starmer as leader of the Labour Party in 2020, the other candidates, Rebecca Long Bailey and Lisa Nandy, signed a pledge[14] promising to expel 'transphobic' members, as did candidates for the deputy leader, Angela Rayner, Rosena Allin-Khan and Dawn Butler, with Butler infamously claiming in a television interview[15] that 'a child is born without sex'. The pledge branded Woman's Place UK and the LGB Alliance as 'trans exclusionist hate groups' and required supporters to 'accept that transwomen are women, trans men are men, and non-binary people are non-binary', and 'accept that there is no material conflict between trans rights and women's rights, and that all transwomen are subject to misogyny and patriarchal oppression'. This was around the same time that my application to re-join the Labour Party was refused due to my feminist views. It appears that many on the liberal Left, not just the politicians, have abandoned the fight for women's rights, or been so cowed by the threat of an accusation of transphobia, that they dare not speak out. For others, transgender identity ideology provides the perfect cloak for their unchecked misogyny. If the left has abandoned women, this should not mean that feminists abandon core tenets of left-wing politics: solidarity, justice and the fair distribution of resources and power. We must reclaim and rebuild, not allow ourselves to be diminished by those who diminish us. We cannot allow feminism to lend respectability to that which we oppose or to those with politics that we abhor.

Resisting sex stereotypes and gender norms is a feminist issue and a trans one too, and yet we are divided between those who think that the answer lies in changing the individual and those who believe that we need to change society, to abolish not entrench gender. How can it be that a body needs to be altered chemically and surgically to fit the prison of gender, rather than the bars of the cells be ripped down? If there are age differences between those who embrace identity politics and those who recognise the solidarity of class, it is because the seeds of Thatcherism had been sown and flourished. Thatcherism saw the end of the post-war consensus and deliberately set out to quash class consciousness. The notion of free choice is simply the domestic version of the free market. Selfism and identity are the twin enemies of solidarity. Just as patriarchy pits women and girls against our sisters in the competition for male regard, capitalism pushes the myth of the meritocracy so that many cannot see the hand of advantage in their achievements. The altruism of identity politics comes easy to those whose lives have offered them choices.

In a win for common sense and decency to victim-survivors of men's violence, in December 2021, the judges' interim Equal Treatment Bench Book (which is a guide to help judges make sure the law is applied in a fair, rather than discriminatory way) identified some circumstances in which witnesses will not be compelled to use the preferred pronouns of defendants which don't accord with their sex. After advising on the use of pre-ferred pronouns for several years, and penalising assault victim Maria MacLachlan for resisting enforced use in court, the revi-sion makes exceptions for those giving evidence about sexual and domestic violence. Stating that 'a victim of domestic abuse or sexual violence at the hands of a trans person may under-standably describe the alleged perpetrator and use pronouns consistent with their gender assigned at birth because that is in accordance with the victim's experience and perception. Artificial steps such as requiring a victim to modify his/her language to disguise this risk interfering with his/her ability to give evidence of a traumatic event.' Whilst some of us may baulk at the use of the phrase 'gender assigned at birth' for reasons that I have explained, and although it remains unclear whether Maria MacLachlan would have been able to use this exemption, it is nevertheless a step in the right direction.

The women of 'Terf Island' are making sure that our voices are heard and that our sex-based rights and protections are not taken away and that children are protected from life-altering and irreversible hormones and surgery. Maya Forstater went to court and established that the belief that sex was immutable was protected in law and 'worthy of respect in a democratic society'.[16] Allison Bailey, a Black, lesbian barrister, took legal action against her chambers Garden Court – who were found to have victimised her and discriminated against her for expressing gender-critical beliefs – and Stonewall, who were not found to have instructed or caused that unlawful conduct but whose tactics and, according to Bailey, malign influence, had been laid bare.[17] Women in Brighton who are current and former service users of the local specialist provider, RISE, have come together as Rise Up, and are fighting for the council to return a contract lost through a commissioning process.[18] As we saw previously, Keira Bell took the Tavistock Clinic to court for failing to properly challenge the decisions she made when she was 16 years old. Though she lost at appeal, Bell says that she does not regret bringing the case, which she said 'shone a light into the dark corners of a medical scandal that is harming children and harmed me.'[19] Sonia Appleby, a psychoanalytical psychotherapist and child safeguarding expert, won an employment tribunal case against the Tavistock and Portman NHS because of the way she was treated after raising concerns about the safety of increasing numbers of children undergoing gender identity treatment.[20] Raquel Rosario Sánchez, a PhD candidate from the Dominican Republic, took Bristol University to court for failing to protect her from bullying for her feminist beliefs (arguably, the university's actions positively aided the bullies). Although she lost the case – the court ruling on the case found that she was not owed a 'duty of care' by the university – the judgment found that she was the victim of 'violent, threatening, intimidating behaviour or language' and that the university had taken an excessively long time to properly respond to her safety concerns.[21] Essex University was forced to apologise after unlawfully no-platforming feminist academics.[22] Julie Bindel sued Pink News for libel and reached a settlement agreeing a joint statement in which Pink News said it had reviewed its editorial process and admitted that if the serious allegations in the article were 'understood to refer to Julie, they would be wholly untrue'.[23] Fair Play for Women won a case requiring the government in England and Wales to change its guidance to people filling out the 2021 census to require people with transgender identities (and who do not hold a Gender Recognition Certificate) to record their actual sex.[24] For Women Scotland fought the Scottish government in Scotland's highest civil court, the Court of Sessions, and secured the interpretations of the words 'woman' and 'man' in the Equality Act as meaning that a woman is someone who is biologically female and a man is someone who is biologically male.[25] Yes, the word 'woman' is taken – and it is ours. And while I'm here, so too is the word 'lesbian'.

Women on Terf Island are fighting back. We are resisting the ideology that threatens to roll back the rights and protections in law and services that our fore-sisters fought hard to achieve and build. Increasing numbers of us are fighting to protect the single-sex services that are still needed because of men's violence against women. It should not be necessary for woman after woman to share how she was abused and the impact that this has had on her to ensure that women's experiences and expertise is taken into account in policy and service provision. The dismissal of decades of survivor voices, supported by specialist practitioners and academics, shows the disregard paid to women's needs.

Brains are not sexed, bodies are, and we are largely, though not solely, shaped by our interactions with the world. We learn personality traits and qualities associated with femininity and masculinity. The concept of gender equality is an oxymoron. Gender is a hierarchy. Sex is the axis of sex-based oppression and gender is the biggest tool in the oppression box. Feminism is ultimately optimistic and offers the hope of change and a better world. Males are not inherently violent and adult males – and females – must always be held accountable for their actions. The movement of women who created services for women who were subjected to men's violence and abuse understood solidarity and their responsibilities to their sisters. We cannot undo their work and we must protect their legacy. As long as men's violence against women is present in society in anything like its current prevalence, we need specialist services for women, girls and children who have been subjected to that violence. To be effective and to offer the best benefit and hope of recovery for some of the most harmed, those services must be single sex. It is not for those who do not need or want those services to deny them to women who do.

Imagine a world without men's violence against women, girls and children. No rape. No partner abuse. No child sex abuse. No prostitution. No women bought or sold. No female genital mutilation. No pornography. No battering. No femicide. Imagine a world without women's subjugation. No sex pay gap. No failure of representation. No sex-role stereotypes. Equal distribution of caring and domestic responsibilities and duties. No concepts of masculinity and femininity. No girls and women should be and do 'x', and boys and men should be and do 'y'. Where women are not from Venus and men are not from Mars. No girl socialised for subservience and servility. No boy socialised to dominate and feel entitled.

Imagine a world where we are all born with equal access to opportunities for growth and development. No deprivation. No inherited privilege. No racism. From each according to their ability, to each according to their need.[26] Imagine a world without men's violence. This is the world that many feminists want to create: a vision of liberation from patriarchal capitalism. Until this world is a reality, we need single-sex spaces for women.

About nia

As I have described in this book, nia took the decision to speak out to protect single-sex services for women, girls and children who had been subjected to men's violence, fully aware that this could be a risk to the organisation's long-term viability.

nia has been delivering services to women and children who have been subjected to men's violence, particularly sexual and domestic violence and abuse, including prostitution, since 1975.

nia delivers a range of services across London, primarily in the East and North of the city. Our services are continually evolving in order to respond to the needs of women who face multiple disadvantage and barriers to accessing services. They currently include:

- East London Rape Crisis for women and girls who have experienced any form of sexual violence – including rape, sexual assault and child sexual abuse – regardless of when it occurred, who it was perpetrated by and whether or not it was reported to the police.

- The Emma Project – a pioneering service for women who are escaping domestic and sexual violence and who use substances problematically.
- Daria House – a refuge for women who have been sexually exploited, with a particular focus on supporting women who have been exploited through involvement in prostitution.
- Community-based advocacy services for women being subjected to domestic violence and abuse.
- The Anita Project – supporting women in prostitution and particularly to exit prostitution.

nia is unapologetically women centred and, as far as I am aware, was the first women's organisation in the country to develop a policy to prioritise women by using the single-sex exceptions lawfully permitted in the Equality Act 2010.

If you have read this and would like to donate to support nia's work, please visit our website at https://niaend ingviolence.org.uk/get-involved/fundraising/

Notes

Chapter 1: What's the Problem?

1 WESC Transgender Equality HC 390 2016-16, 14 January 2016.

2 US Institute of Medicine Committee on Understanding the Biology of Sex and Gender Differences; Wizemann TM, Pardue ML, editors. (2001) Sex Begins in the Womb. In *Exploring the Biological Contributions to Human Health: Does Sex Matter?* Washington, DC: National Academies Press. Available from: https://www.ncbi.nlm.nih.gov/books/NBK222 286/

3 Office for National Statistics (2020) All data related to Domestic abuse in England and Wales overview: November 2020. Available at: https://www.ons.gov.uk/peoplepopulationandcommunity/crimeandjustice/bulletins/domesticabuseinenglandandwalesoverview/november2020/relateddata

4 Office for National Statistics (2020) Domestic abuse and the criminal justice system, England and Wales: November 2020. Available at: https://www.ons.gov.uk/peoplepopulationandcommunity/crimeandjustice/articles/domesticabuseandthecriminaljusticesystemenglandandwales/november2020

5 Office for National Statistics (2020) Nature of sexual assault by rape or penetration, England and Wales: year ending March 2020. Available at: https://www.ons.gov.uk/peoplepopulationandcommunity/crimeandjustice/articles/natureofsexualassaultbyrapeorpenetrationenglandandwales/yearendingmarch2020

6 House of Commons Home Affairs Committee (2017) Prostitution.

Available at: https://publications.parliament.uk/pa/cm201617/cmselect /cmhaff/26/26.pdf

7 Office for National Statistics (2020) Child sexual abuse in England and Wales: year ending March 2019. Available at: https://www.ons.gov.uk /peoplepopulationandcommunity/crimeandjustice/articles/childsexua labuseinenglandandwales/yearendingmarch2019

8 Sardinha, H., Maheu-Giroux, M., Stockl, H., Meyer, S.R. and Garcia-Moreno, C. (2022) Global, regional, and national prevalence estimates of physical or sexual, or both, intimate partner violence against women in 2018. *The Lancet*, 399 (10327), 803–13.

9 Liz Kelly describes how the concept of a conducive context arose when she was researching trafficking in Central Asia and how, in order to address trafficking, it was necessary to address not only those victimised or potentially victimised and those involved in organised crime, but to look also at 'interconnecting social, political and economic conditions within which exploitative operators profit from the misfortunes of others'. Kelly, L. (2016) 'The Conducive Context of Violence Against Women and Girls'. *Discover Society*, Issue 30.

10 Walby, S. (1990) *Theorising Patriarchy*. Oxford: Blackwell Publishers.

11 Large houses, usually with support staff working in them where women and their children can go to stay if they need to do so to escape domestic violence and abuse. Some countries call them women's shelters, but this term isn't really used in the UK.

12 An ideology is a set of ideas or beliefs, often underpinning how supporters set out to deal with an issue. When I talk about gender ideology, I'm talking about beliefs that roles, rights and responsibilities for people should reflect their sex: these are gender stereotypes. And if I talk about transgender ideology, it is gender ideology combined with a belief that you have an innate gender, something that you were born with, that predisposes you to certain roles and responsibilities, and that this is more important in determining who you are than your sex is.

13 Legislation.gov.uk. Equality Act 2010. Explanatory Notes: Commentary on Sections Part 16, Schedule 3, Part 7: Separate and single services. Available at: https://www.legislation.gov.uk/ukpga/2010/15/notes/divis ion/3/16/20/7

14 Equality and Human Rights Commission (2022) Separate and single-sex service providers: a guide on the Equality Act sex and gender reassignment provisions. Available at: https://www.equalityhumanrights.com /en/advice-and-guidance/separate-and-single-sex-service-providers-gu ide-equality-act-sex-and-gender

15 Although I talk about women victim-survivors of men's violence, women's support organisations do work with lesbians. Physical violence may be less common in lesbian relationships, though abuse is not completely absent. In addition, being a lesbian does not completely protect a woman from men's violence; organisations like Rape Crisis support women regardless of how long ago they were abused, which could have been when they were a child, so the adult woman's sexuality would not have made a difference.

16 British Triathlon (2022) Statement from British Triathlon Federation, 6 July. Available at: https://www.britishtriathlon.org/news/statement-from-british-triathlon-federation_17073

17 A Plea for Third Spaces for Transmen and Transwomen. Available at: https://www.change.org/p/boris-johnson-a-plea-for-third-spaces-for-transgender-men-and-women

18 Burgess, K. (2015) Greer defends view on what does and doesn't 'make you a f*****g woman'. *The Times*, 27 October 2015.

19 Curzon, G.N. (undated leaflet published between 1910 and 1914) Fifteen Good Reasons Against the Grant of Female Suffrage. Available at: https://digital.nls.uk/suffragettes/sources/source-24.html

20 For example, Kellie/Frank Maloney, 'I am a woman born into a man's body but I had to deny who I was.' In Cavendish, L. (2015) Kellie Maloney, formerly Frank, on being a heterosexual woman. *The Times*, 22 August 2015. Available at https://www.thetimes.co.uk/article/kellie-maloney-formerly-frank-on-being-a-heterosexual-woman-mhpz2q66w7h. India Willoughby, 'It is about being born into the wrong body, which I was.' In Nicholas, S. (2016) Transgender journalist India Willoughby talks about the double life she led for decades. *Express*, 19 October. Available at https://www.express.co.uk/life-style/life/722571/India-Willoughby-transgender-surgery-ITV-journalist-UK-life-LGBT. Jazz Jennings, 'Ever since I could form coherent thoughts, I knew I was a girl trapped inside a boy's body.' In Jazz Jennings: When I First Knew I Was Transgender (2016) *TIME*, 31 May. Available at: https://time.com/4350574/jazz-jennings-transgender/

21 Kravitz, M. (2020) The Gender Binary Is a Tool of White Supremacy. Medium, 14 July. Available at https://aninjusticemag.com/the-gender-binary-is-a-tool-of-white-supremacy-db89d0bc9044. Phipps, Alison (2019) The fight against sexual violence. *Soundings: A Journal of Politics and Culture*, 71, 62–74.

22 Judith Butler, in Gleeson, J. (2021) Interview: Judith Butler: 'We need to rethink the category of woman'. *The Guardian*, 21 September. Available

at   https://www.theguardian.com/lifeandstyle/2021/sep/07/judith-but ler-interview-gender

23 Stock examines the gamete, chromosome and cluster (morphological characteristics) accounts and concludes that there is 'no serious challenge to the idea of two natural, pre-given sexes'. Stock, K. (2021) *Material Girls: Why reality matters for feminism*. London: Fleet, pp. 44–75.

24 Rippon, G. (2019) *The Gendered Brain*. London: Bodley Head.

25 Fine, C. (2011) *Delusions of Gender*. London: Icon Books.

26 Kneeskern, E.E. and Reeder, P.A. (2022) Examining the impact of fiction literature on children's gender stereotypes. *Current Psychology*, 41, 1472–85.

27 Fox, G. (2019) Meet the neuroscientist shattering the myth of the gendered brain. *The Observer*, 24 February. Available at: https://www.the guardian.com/science/2019/feb/24/meet-the-neuroscientist-shattering -the-myth-of-the-gendered-brain-gina-rippon

28 Fine, *Delusions of Gender*, pp. 236 and 237.

29 The Cleveland Clinic offers a useful description of gender reassignment treatments. Cleveland Clinic: Gender Affirmation (Confirmation) or Sex Reassignment Surgery. Available at: https://my.clevelandclinic.org/hea lth/treatments/21526-gender-affirmation-confirmation-or-sex-reassign ment-surgery

30 Ibid.

31 Crane, C. (2016) Phalloplasty and metoidioplasty – overview and post-operative considerations. Transgender Care. Available at: https://transc are.ucsf.edu/guidelines/phalloplasty

32 James, S.E., Herman, J.L., Rankin, S., et al. (2016) *The Report of the 2015 US Transgender Survey*. Washington, DC: National Center for Transgender Equality.

33 Sineath, R.C., Woodyatt, C., Sanchez, T., et al (2016). Determinants of and barriers to hormonal and surgical treatment receipt among transgender people. *Transgender Health*, 1 (1), 129–36.

34 Beckwith, N., Reisner, S.L., Zaslow, S., et al. (2017) Factors associated with gender-affirming surgery and age of hormone therapy initiation among transgender adults. *Transgender Health*, 2 (1), 156–64.

35 Ibid.

36 Strudwick, P. (2015) This trans woman kept her beard and couldn't be happier. Buzzfeed, 16 July 2016. Available at: https://www.buzzfeed .com/patrickstrudwick/this-transgender-woman-has-a-full-beard-and -she-couldnt-be-h

37 St James, E. (2020) The Assimilationist, or: On the unexpected cost of

passing as a trans woman. Vox, 19 February. Available at: https://www. vox.com/the-highlight/2020/2/12/21075683/trans-coming-out-cost-of-womanhood-pink-tax

38 Sellberg, K. (2012) Transgender identity and passing authentically. In: Cooley, D. and Harrison, K (eds) *Pro-Passing, Transgender Identity and Literature: (Post-)transsexual Politics and Poetics of Passing.* Farnham: Ashgate.

39 Colliver, B. and Silvestru, M. (2020) The role of (in)visibility in hate crime targeting transgender people. *Criminology and Criminal Justice,* 22 (2), 235–53.

40 Kilikita, J. (2021) As a trans woman, I understand the pressure to pass. But it's holding us back. Refinery29, 19 November. Available at: https:// www.refinery29.com/en-gb/passing-as-a-trans-woman

41 Some former partners of males who have transitioned refer to themselves as trans widows. Though as one woman, who does not like the term, told me, it might have been easier being a widow; if she had been a widow and her partner had died, her need to grieve the loss of her partner would have been understood and supported.

42 'An umbrella term to describe people whose gender is not the same as, or does not sit comfortably with, the sex they were assigned at birth. Trans people may describe themselves using one or more of a wide variety of terms, including (but not limited to) transgender, transsexual, gender-queer (GQ), gender-fluid, non-binary, gender-variant, crossdresser, genderless, agender, nongender, third gender, bi-gender, trans man, trans woman, trans masculine, trans feminine and neutrois.' https://www.stonewall.org.uk/help-advice/faqs-and-glossary/list-lgbtq-terms

43 Sex is determined at conception and this is reflected in our chromosomes. The development of secondary sex characteristics (internal and external reproductive organs) is determined by hormones. Where there are developmental differences which may mean that a person's sex is difficult to determine because things look different, that person is still either female or male. Having DSDs can cause lots of issues for people who are affected but it is wrong, in my opinion, to bring those issues into the arena of transgender rights activism. Some people with DSDs, many of whom may not have chosen to broadcast their personal medical issues, are increasingly objecting to being levered into the debate.

44 Anne Fausto-Sterling suggested that the prevalence of intersex people was about 1.7% of the population. This calculation included people with Klinefelter syndrome, Turner syndrome and late-onset adrenal

hyperplasia. If the term intersex is used only to apply to people whose chromosomes are inconsistent with their genitals, or where their genitals are ambiguous, the prevalence of intersex people is almost 100% lower: 0.018%. From Sax, L. (2002) How common is intersex? A response to Anne Fausto-Sterling. *Journal of Sex Research*, 39 (3), 174–8.

45 This is the way I will conceptualise transphobia in the book, not the way it can be used to describe anyone critical of or questioning gender identity ideology.

46 'While I believe we have to stay true to the core of the history of our sector, we have to have a response that is not based on policing people's sexual characteristics in order for them to access a service. . . . We do have to respond to the permission, if you like, to identify as a gender without that being scrutinised in terms of only biology, because it is not only biology'. Janet McDermott, WAFE, WESC, 22 May 2019.

47 There are lots of definitional issues surrounding the word femicide, and I explore these in my PhD thesis. For now, it's most appropriate to say that, while there is a lot of overlap in the terms 'femicide' and 'men's fatal violence against women', they are not exactly the same.

48 Crenshaw, K. (1991) Mapping the margins: Intersectionality, identity politics and violence against women of colour. *Stanford Law Review*, 43 (6), 1241–99.

Chapter 2: Sex Inequality

1 Irish Central (2022) On This Day: Irish revolutionary Countess Constance Markievicz was born, in London, in 1868. Available at: https://www.iris hcentral.com/roots/history/countess-constance-markievicz-irish-revol utionary

2 TheyWorkForYou: Viscountess Nancy Astor. Available at: https://www .theyworkforyou.com/mp/16515/nancy_astor/plymouth%2C_sutton

3 Rodrigues, J. (2012) 30 years ago: El Vino's treatment of women drinkers ruled unlawful. *The Guardian*, 15 November. Available at: https://www .theguardian.com/theguardian/from-the-archive-blog/2012/nov/15/el -vino-women-ban-fleet-street-1982

4 Casemine, *DPP v. Morgan*. United Kingdom House of Lords, 30 April 1975. Available at: https://www.casemine.com/judgement/uk/5a8ff 8ca60d03e7f57ecd7a3. Judgments – Morgans v. Director of Public Prosecutions (On Appeal from a Divisional Court of The Queen's Bench Division).

5 Legal Information Institute, *R. v. r.* Available at: https://www.law.corne ll.edu/women-and-justice/resource/r_v_r

6 IFPA, History of Abortion in Ireland, 2018. Available at: https://www.if
   pa.ie/advocacy/abortion-in-ireland-legal-timeline/
7 Messerly, A. (2022) Abortion laws by state: Legal status of abortion
   changing day-by-day after Roe v. Wade overturned. Politico, 6 July.
   Available at: https://www.politico.com/news/2022/07/06/abortion-laws
   -states-roe-overturned-00044127
8 Gov.uk. The Equality Act. Available at: https://www.gov.uk/guidance
   /equality-act-2010-guidance
9 Valisce, S. (2017) My work as a prostitute led me to oppose decriminalisation. BBC, 2 October. Available at: https://www.bbc.co.uk/news/maga
   zine-41349301
10 Norak, S. and Kraus, I. (2018) 'Never again! Surviving liberalised prostitution in Germany', Dignity: A Journal of Analysis of Exploitation and
   Violence, 3 (3), art. 5. https://doi.org/10.23860/dignity.2018.03.03.05
11 Sönmezocak, E.B. (2021) A feminist response against impunity in gender
   based violence: whom the presumption of innocence protects? Yeditepe
   Üniversitesi Hukuk Fakültesi Dergisi, 18, 377–407.
12 Office for National Statistics (2020) All data related to Domestic abuse
   in England and Wales overview: November 2020. Available at: https://
   www.ons.gov.uk/peoplepopulationandcommunity/crimeandjustice/bul
   letins/domesticabuseinenglandandwalesoverview/november2020/relat
   eddata
13 Walby, S. and Towers, J. (2017) Measuring violence to end violence:
   mainstreaming gender. Journal of Gender-Based Violence, 1 (1),
   11–31.
14 Office for National Statistics (2020) Domestic abuse and the criminal
   justice system, England and Wales: November 2020. Available at:
   https://www.ons.gov.uk/peoplepopulationandcommunity/crimeand
   justice/articles/domesticabuseandthecriminaljusticesystemenglandand
   wales/november2020
15 Office for National Statistics (2020) Nature of sexual assault by rape or
   penetration, England and Wales: year ending March 2020. Available
   at: https://www.ons.gov.uk/peoplepopulationandcommunity/crimeand
   justice/articles/natureofsexualassaultbyrapeorpenetrationenglandand
   wales/yearendingmarch2020
16 Brooks-Gordon, B., Mai, N. and Sanders, T. (2015) Calculating the
   number of sex workers and contribution to non-observed economy in
   the UK. Office for National Statistics. Available at: https://eprints.bbk.ac
   .uk/id/eprint/21670/
17 Parke, S. and Karsna, K. (2019) Measuring the scale and changing

nature of child sexual abuse. Centre of Expertise on Child Sexual Abuse. Available at: https://www.csacentre.org.uk/csa-centre-prodv2/assets/File/Scale%20and%20nature%20update%202019.pdf

18 Kimmel, M.S. (2002) 'Gender symmetry' in domestic violence: a substantive and methodological research review. *Violence Against Women*, 8 (11), 1332–63.

19 Dobash, R.E. and Dobash, P.D. (1998) *Rethinking Violence Against Women*. Thousand Oaks, CA: Sage.

20 Hester, M. (2009) *Who Does What to Whom? Gender and Domestic Violence Perpetrators*. University of Bristol in association with the Northern Rock Foundation.

21 Ingala Smith, K. (2021) *Sex differences in intimate partner homicide (England and Wales) April 2009 to March 2020*. Available at: https://kareningalasmith.com/2021/08/23/sex-differences-in-intimate-partner-homicide-england-and-wales-april-2009-to-march-2020/

22 Office for National Statistics (2021) Homicide in England and Wales: year ending March 2020. Available at: https://www.ons.gov.uk/peoplepopulationandcommunity/crimeandjustice/articles/homicideinenglandandwales/yearendingmarch2020

23 Ibid.

24 Centre for Women's Justice (2021) *Women Who Kill: How the State Criminalises Women We Might Otherwise Be Burying*. London: CWJ. Available at https://www.centreforwomensjustice.org.uk/women-who-kill.

25 Ibid.

26 Kelly, L. (1987) The continuum of sexual violence. In: Hanmer, J. and Maynard, M. (eds) *Women, Violence and Social Control* (Explorations in Sociology 23). Basingstoke: Palgrave Macmillan.

27 Imkaan and EVAW (2020) *Joint Briefing: Adjournment Debate: Black Women and Domestic Abuse*. Available at: https://www.endviolenceagainstwomen.org.uk/wp-content/uploads/Joint-Briefing-for-Meg-Hillier-MP-Debate-EVAW-Imkaan.pdf

28 Siddiqui, H. (2014) Violence against minority women: tackling domestic violence, forced marriage and 'honour' based violence. PhD thesis, University of Warwick.

29 Hinsliff, G. (2008) Harman and Law Lord clash over wife killers. *The Observer*, 9 November 2008. Available at: https://www.theguardian.com/politics/2008/nov/09/harriet-harman-defence-of-provocation

30 Gracia, E. and Merlo, J. (2016) Intimate partner violence against women and the Nordic paradox. *Social Science and Medicine*, 157, 27–30.

31 Stonewall (n.d.) *The Truth about Trans. How many trans people are there in Britain at the moment?* Available at: https://www.stonewall.org. uk/truth-about-trans#trans-people-britain

32 Varrella, S. (2022) Share of people identifying as transgender, gender fluid, non-binary, or other ways worldwide as of 2021, by country. Statista. Available at https://www.statista.com/statistics/1269778/gen der-identity-worldwide-country/

33 Flores, A.R., Herman, J.L., Gates, G.J., et al. (2016) *How Many Adults Identify as Transgender in the United States?* Los Angeles, CA: The Williams Institute.

34 Nolan, I.T., Kuhner, C.J. and Dy, G.W. (2019) Demographic and temporal trends in transgender identities and gender confirming surgery. *Translational Andrology and Urology*, 8 (3), 184–90.

35 Dhejne, C., Lichtenstein, P., Boman, M., et al. (2011) Long-term follow-up of transsexual persons undergoing sex reassignment surgery: cohort study in Sweden. *PLoS ONE*, 6(2), e16885.

36 MurrayBlackburnMackenzie. (2021) Long-term follow-up of transsexual persons undergoing sex reassignment surgery: cohort study in Sweden: a review of Dhejne et al.'s findings on criminal convictions. Available at: https://mbmpolicy.files.wordpress.com/2021/04/mbm-briefing-on-dhjene-et-al.-april-2021-1.pdf

37 A WESC report repeated unreliable claims about transgender young people and suicide risk; the claim that transgender people are at increased risk of murder is frequently made and addressed in this book. Specialist refuge providers have lost contracts because of a focus on women.

38 Transgender Trend (2016) A scientist reviews transgender suicide stats. Available at: https://www.transgendertrend.com/a-scientist-reviews-tra nsgender-suicide-stats/

39 Fair Play For Women (2018) Trans suicide facts and myths. Available at: https://fairplayforwomen.com/suicide/

Chapter 3: Standing on the Shoulders of Giants

1 Hague, G. (2021) *History and Memories of the Domestic Violence Movement*. Bristol: Policy Press.

2 The group that became Southall Black Sisters was established in West London by women who had been active in anti-racist and anti-fascist protests against the National Front, including that in which the activist Blair Peach was killed in 1979. Lee Eggleston and Sheila Coates, who set up what became South Essex Rape and Incest Crisis Centre, have spoken

about how sexual harassment at CND meetings was instrumental in helping them conceptualise sexual violence as a collective experience. These were most often distinct services reflecting the interests – and lack of resources needed to run bigger organisations – of the women who set them up, but women understood that all forms of men's violence against women were linked.

3 Hague, *History and Memories of the Domestic Violence Movement*, p. 19.
4 Fife Rape and Sexual Assault Centre (n.d.) *The Rape Crisis Movement*. Available at: https://www.frasac.org.uk/about-rape-crisis-movement/
5 Johnson, G., Ribar, D.C. and Zhu, A. (2017) Women's homelessness: international evidence on causes, consequences, coping and policies. Melbourne Institute Working Paper No. 7/17.
6 Shelter (2021) *Fobbed Off: The barriers preventing women accessing housing and homelessness support, and the women-centred approach needed to overcome them.* Available at: https://england.shelter.org.uk/professional_resources/policy_and_research/policy_library/fobbed_off_the_barriers_preventing_women_accessing_housing_and_homelessness_support
7 United Nations, Declaration on the Elimination of Violence against Women, 2003. Available at: https://www.un.org/en/genocideprevention/documents/atrocity-crimes/Doc.21_declaration%20elimination%20vaw.pdf
8 Southall Black Sisters (2018) SBS's victory against Ealing Council. Available at: https://southallblacksisters.org.uk/news/sbss-victory-against-ealing-council/
9 See examples including Monklands Women's Aid, Motherwell District Women's Aid, North Lanarkshire Women's Aid and RISE later in the chapter.
10 I'll be looking at nia's work to protect single-sex services in chapter 5.
11 Gov.uk (2016) Press release: Government announces new clause to be inserted into grant agreements. Available at https://www.gov.uk/government/news/government-announces-new-clause-to-be-inserted-into-grant-agreements
12 Davidson, G. (2021) North Lanarkshire council accused of 'callous decision' to withdraw funding for women's aid services. *The Scotsman*, 26 February. Available at: https://www.scotsman.com/news/politics/north-lanarkshire-council-accused-of-callous-decision-to-withdraw-funding-for-womens-aid-services-3147513
13 Learmonth, A. (2021) Nicola Sturgeon says fears over reform of GRA

are 'not valid'. Holyrood, 10 September. Available at: https://www.holy
rood.com/news/view,nicola-sturgeon-says-fears-over-reform-of-gen
der-recognition-act-are-not-valid

14 Vancouver Rape Relief and Women's Shelter (n.d.) Nixon v. Vancouver
Rape Relief Society: Chronology of events. Available at: https://rape
liefshelter.bc.ca/nixon-v-vancouver-rape-relief-society-chronology-of
-events/

15 The Supporting People Quality Assessment Framework (QAF) did not
specifically assess a service's ability to meet the needs of women fleeing
abusive men.

16 Coy, M. and Kelly, L. (2011) *Islands in the Stream: An Evaluation of Four
London Independent Domestic Violence Advocacy Schemes.* London:
London Metropolitan University.

Chapter 4: What Difference Does it Make?

1 Imkaan and EVAW (2020) *Joint Briefing: Adjournment Debate: Black
Women and Domestic Abuse.*

2 Women and Equalities Committee, Transgender Equality HC 390 2016-
16, 14 January 2016, para. 121, p. 30.

3 Monckton-Smith, J. (2020) Intimate partner femicide: using Foucauldian
analysis to track an eight stage progression to homicide. *Violence Against
Women*, 26 (11), 1267–85.

4 Monckton Smith, J. (2021) *In Control.* London: Bloomsbury Circus.

5 Femicide Census (2019) UK Femicides 2009–2018. Available at: https://
www.femicidecensus.org/wp-content/uploads/2020/11/Femicide-Cen
sus-10-year-report.pdf

6 Hilton, E.N. and Lundberg, T.R. (2021) Transgender women in the
female category of sport: perspectives on testosterone suppression and
performance advantage. *Sports Medicine*, 51, 199–214.

7 Women's Aid (2021) *The Domestic Abuse Report 2021.* Available at:
https://www.womensaid.org.uk/wp-content/uploads/2021/09/The-Do
mestic-Abuse-Report-2021-The-Annual-Audit-Revised-2021.pdf

8 Turner, E., Medina, J. and Brown, G. (2019) Dashing hopes? The predic-
tive accuracy of domestic abuse risk assessment by police. *The British
Journal of Criminology*, 59 (5), 1013–34.

9 James-Hanman, D. (2018) Whose movement is it anyway? Reflections
from the field. In Holt, S., Øverlien, C. and Devaney, J. (eds) *Responding
to Domestic Violence: Emerging Challenges for Policy, Practice and
Research in Europe.* London: Jessica Kingsley Publishers.

10 Lima, A.A., Fiszman, A., Marques-Portella, C., et al. (2010) The Impact

of Tonic Immobility Reaction on the Prognosis of Posttraumatic Stress Disorder. *Journal of Psychiatric Research*, 44(4), 224–8.

11 Widom, C., Czaja, S.J. and Dutton, M.A. (2008) Childhood victimisation and lifetime revictimisation. *Child Abuse & Neglect*, 32 (8), 785–96.

12 Classen, C., Gronskaya Palesh, O. and Aggarwal, R. (2005) Sexual revictimisation: a review of the empirical literature. *Trauma Violence Abuse*, 6 (2), 103–29.

13 ONS (2017) Impact of child abuse on later life, Crime Survey for England and Wales, year ending March 2016. Available at: https://www.ons.gov.uk/peoplepopulationandcommunity/crimeandjustice/adhocs/007527 impactofchildabuseonlaterlifecrimesurveyforenglandandwalesyear endingmarch2016

14 Kinnell, H. (2008) *Violence and Sex Work in Britain*. London: Taylor & Francis. Church, S., Henderson, M., Barnard, M. and Hart, G. (2001) Violence by clients towards female prostitutes in different work settings: questionnaire survey. *BMJ*, 322 (7285), 524–5. Campbell, R. and Stoops, S. (2010) Taking sex workers seriously: treating violence against sex workers as hate crime in Liverpool. *Research for Sex Work (Special edition on Violence Against Sex Workers)*, 12, 9–10.

15 Ward, H., Day, S. and Weber, J. (1999) Risky business: health and safety in the sex industry over a 9 year period. *Journal of Sexually Transmitted Infections*, 75 (5), 340–3.

16 Farley, M. and Barkan, H. (1998) Prostitution, violence, and posttraumatic stress disorder. *Women Health*, 27 (3), 37–49.

17 Cited in van der Kolk, B. (2014) *The Body Keeps the Score*. London: Penguin.

18 Ibid., p. 60.

19 Ibid., p. 43.

20 Hewitt, R. (2015) When I was raped, it was female-only spaces that helped me recover. *New Statesman*, 24 February. Available at: https://www.newstatesman.com/politics/2015/02/when-i-was-raped-it-was-female-only-spaces-helped-me-recover

21 van der Kolk, *The Body Keeps the Score*, p. 134.

22 I share some quotes from women who have used sexual and domestic violence services, about how important woman-only space was to them, in chapter 5.

23 Oasis Women's Refuge in Kent state on their website: 'The Oasis Women's Refuge is a welcoming and diverse place to stay – we welcome women of all backgrounds, races and orientations. Oasis welcomes trans-women

who have experienced domestic abuse.' Available at: https://www.oasis daservice.org/oasis-refuge

24   Quinn, M.E. (2010) *Open Minds Open Doors*. Massachusetts: The Network/La Red. Available at http://www.ncdsv.org/images/TheNet workLaRed_OpenMindsOpenDoors_2010.pdf identifies the following services as inclusive of males with transgender identies in their women's services in Massachusetts: Reach, in Waltham; HAWC in Salem; Renewal House in Boston; New Hope in South-eastern Massachusetts, Harbour COV in Chelsea.

25   Ray Blanchard, University of Toronto, researched autogynephilia and categorised males who identified as women into two groups: androphilic (homosexual) and autogynephilic. The categorisation is supported by many researchers but often strongly criticised by transgender activists. In Perry, L. (2019) What is autogynephilia? An interview with Dr Ray Blanchard. Quillette. Available at: https://quillette.com/2019/11/06/wh at-is-autogynephilia-an-interview-with-dr-ray-blanchard/. Blanchard said 'I very much doubt that the prevalence of autogynephilia per se, or the prevalence of autogynephilic gender dysphoria, has increased. I think that what has changed is the proportion of autogynephilic trans who have "come out"', and 'When I looked at the relative numbers of autogynephilic and androphilic gender-dysphoric males back in 1987, the autogynephilic cases were already a majority, approaching 60 percent. The proportion had reached 75 percent by 2010, and it might be even higher now.'

26   Rosario Sánchez, R. (2022) The remarkable poise of Allison Bailey. The Critic, 17 May. Available at: https://thecritic.co.uk/the-remarkable-poise-of-allison-bailey/

27   Faulkner, D. (2021) Maya Forstater: Woman wins tribunal appeal over transgender tweets. BBC, 10 June. Available at https://www.bbc.co.uk/news/uk-57426579

28   BBC (2022) Raquel Rosario Sanchez loses legal case over trans rights protests. BBC, 21 April. Available at: https://www.bbc.co.uk/news/uk-england-bristol-61179937

29   BBC News (2021) NHS child gender identity clinic whistle-blower wins tribunal. BBC, 5 September. Available at: https://www.bbc.co.uk/news/uk-58453250

30   Kelly, J. (2021) Kathleen Stock – free speech and fear on campus. *Financial Times*, 5 November. Available at https://www.ft.com/content/9504baa4-5cf9-40b5-87b5-04d24f19f2b6

31   Moore, S. (2020) Why I had to leave The Guardian. UnHerd, 25

November. Available at: https://unherd.com/2020/11/why-i-had-to-leave-the-guardian/

32 Bindel, J. (2021) Trans activism's war on solidarity. UnHerd, 15 October. Available at: https://unherd.com/2021/10/trans-activisms-war-on-solidarity/

33 Hirst, A. and Rinne, A. (2012) The impact of changes in commissioning and funding on women-only services. Equality and Human Rights Commission. Research Report 86.

34 Women's National Commission on Women-only Services (2010).

35 Smith, N., Dogaru, C. and Ellis, F. (2015) A survey of adult survivors of child sexual abuse and their experience of support services. University Campus Suffolk.

36 Aurora New Dawn (2022) By and for women. Available at: https://www.aurorand.org.uk/wp-content/uploads/2022/03/By-Women-for-Women.pdf

37 Turell, S.C. (1999) Seeking help for same-sex relationship abuses. *Journal of Gay & Lesbian Social Services*, 10 (2), 35–49.

38 Sex Matters (2022) Why single-sex services matter: privacy, dignity, fairness and choice. Available at: URL to be supplied when report is released.

39 Didlaw (2022) Sarah Summers: press release, 3 May. Available at: https://didlaw.com/sarah-summers-press-release-3-may-2022

Chapter 5: Looking Beyond

1 Ditum, S. (2018) Labour's 'woman' problem. *The Spectator*, 9 March. Available at: https://www.spectator.co.uk/article/labour-s-woman-problem

2 Institute for Government (2019) Gender balance in parliament. Available at: https://www.instituteforgovernment.org.uk/publication/gender/parliament

3 Samuelson, K. (2022) Labour and the end of all-women shortlists. The Week, 8 March. Available at: https://www.theweek.co.uk/news/politics/956008/labour-and-all-women-shortlists

4 Ministry of Justice (2018) Statistics on Women and the Criminal Justice System 2017, 29 November, p 5. Available at: https://assets.publishing.service.gov.uk/government/uploads/system/uploads/attachment_data/file/759770/women-criminal-justice-system-2017.pdf

5 Ministry of Justice (2020) Statistics on Women and the Criminal Justice System 2019, 26 November. Available at: https://assets.publishing.service.gov.uk/government/uploads/system/uploads/attachment_data/file/938360/statistics-on-women-and-the-criminal-justice-system-2019.pdf

6 Ministry of Justice (2018) Female Offender Strategy. Available at: https://assets.publishing.service.gov.uk/government/uploads/system/uploads/attachment_data/file/719819/female-offender-strategy.pdf

7 Prison Reform Trust (2017) Counted Out: Black, Asian and minority ethnic women in the criminal justice system. Available at: https://prisonreformtrust.org.uk/publication/counted-out-black-asian-and-minority-ethnic-women-in-the-criminal-justice-system

8 Prison Service Instruction on Care and Management of Transsexual Prisoners (PSI 07/2011).

9 House of Commons (2018) Transgender Prisoners. Briefing Paper Number 07420. Available at: https://researchbriefings.files.parliament.uk/documents/CBP-7420/CBP-7420.pdf

10 Sky News (2015) Transgender Tara Hudson Moved to Female Jail. Available at: https://news.sky.com/story/transgender-tara-hudson-moved-to-female-jail-10341295

11 Allison, E. and Pidd, H. (2015) Second transgender prisoner found dead in male jail. *The Guardian*, 1 December. Available at: https://www.theguardian.com/society/2015/dec/01/second-trans-prisoner-joanne-latham-apparently-takes-own-life-in-male-jail

12 Newcomen, N. (2016) Independent investigation into the death of Ms Joanne Latham a prisoner at HMP Woodhill on 27 November 2015. Prison and Probation Ombudsman. Available at: https://www.ppo.gov.uk/app/uploads/2016/09/L215-15-Death-of-Ms-Joanne-Latham-Woodhill-27-11-2016-SID-31-40.pdf

13 Ministry of Justice (2021) HMPPS Offender Equalities Report 2020/21. Available at https://assets.publishing.service.gov.uk/government/uploads/system/uploads/attachment_data/file/1048255/HMPPS_Offender_Equalities_2020-21_FINAL_Revision.pdf

14 Keep Prisons Single Sex. How Many Males Are in Women's Prisons? Available at: https://kpssinfo.org/how-many-males-are-in-womens-prisons/

15 Women and Equalities Committee, Transgender Equality HC 390 2016-16, 14 January 2016, p. 67.

16 British Psychological Society (2015) Written evidence submitted to the Women and Equalities Committee's Transgender Equality Inquiry. Available at: http://data.parliament.uk/WrittenEvidence/CommitteeEvidence.svc/EvidenceDocument/Women%20and%20Equalities/Transgender%20Equality/written/19471.html

17 https://www.nbcnews.com/feature/nbc-out/transgender-women-are-nearly-always-incarcerated-men-s-putting-many-n1142436

18 https://www.prisonpolicy.org/blog/2022/03/31/transgender_incarceration/

19 https://www.latimes.com/california/story/2021-04-05/california-prisons-consider-gender-identity-housing-requests

20 *Janine Chandler, Krystal Gonzalez, Tomiekia Johnson, Nadia Romero v. California Dept of Correction and Rehabilitation*, 2021.

21 Phoenix, J. (2021) A woman's place is not in prison. Transcript of speech at WPUK meeting held on 27 October. Available at: https://jop hoenix.substack.com/p/a-womans-place-is-not-in-prison?s=r

22 House of Commons Justice Committee (2013) Women Offenders: after the Corston Report.

23 Prison Reform Trust (2017) 'There's a reason we're in trouble'. Available at: https://prisonreformtrust.org.uk/publication/theres-a-reason-were -in-trouble-domestic-abuse-as-a-driver-to-womens-offending/

24 Law Society Gazette (2022) Female inmate tells of sex assault by trans prisoner. 18 January. Available at: https://www.lawsociety.ie/gazette /top-stories/2021/12-december/ex-inmate-gives-account-of-sex-assa ult-by-trans-prisoner

25 The Transgender Case Board is the body of agencies that manages decisions on where transgender offenders are placed.

26 Cole, W. (2019) Transgender murderer, 23, is moved back to all-male jail after 'romping with a naked female inmate weeks after being moved to women's prison'. MailOnline, 3 June. Available at: https://www.daily mail.co.uk/news/article-7097351/Trans-murderer-23-moved-male-ja il-romping-naked-female-inmate.html

27 Ministry of Justice (2020) Freedom of Information Act (FOIA) Request – 200513008. Available at: https://assets.publishing.service.gov.uk /government/uploads/system/uploads/attachment_data/file/902685 /FOI_200513008_assaults_involving_transgender_prisoners.doc

28 Brown, D. (2020) Seven sex attacks in women's jails by transgender convicts. *The Times*, 11 May. Available at: https://www.thetimes.co .uk/article/seven-sex-attacks-in-womens-jails-by-transgender-convic ts-cx9m8zqpg

29 UK Parliament, Question for Ministry of Justice from Baroness McDonagh. Tabled 21 April 2020. Answered 5 May 2020. Available at https://questions-statements.parliament.uk/written-questions/deta il/2020-04-21/HL3198

30 Gov.uk (2022) Prison population figures. Available at: https://www.gov .uk/government/publications/prison-population-figures-2022

31 Morton, J.A. (2019) Scottish history of trans equality activism. In Burns, C. (ed.) *Trans Britain*. London: Unbound, p. 240.

32 Cook, J. (2020) The dividing lines over Scotland's gender laws. BBC, 11 February. Available at: https://www.bbc.co.uk/news/uk-scotland-5144 5579

33 Matrix Chambers (2021) High Court Gives Judgment on Policy Regarding Transgender Prisoners. Available at: https://www.matrix law.co.uk/judgments/high-court-gives-judgment-on-policy-regarding -transgender-prisoners/

34 Pleace, N., Fitzpatrick, S. Johnson, S., Quilgars, D. and Sanderson, D. (2008) *Statutory Homelessness in England: The Experience of Families and 16–17 Year Olds*. London: Department of Community and Local Government.

35 Mayock, P., Bretherton, J. and Baptista, I. (2016) Women's homelessness and domestic violence – (in)visible interactions. In Mayock, P. and Bretherton, J. (eds) *Women's Homelessness in Europe*. London: Palgrave Macmillan, pp. 127–54.

36 Wilsnack, S.C., Vogeltanz, N.D., Klassen, A.D. and Harris, T.R. (1997) Childhood sexual abuse and women's substance abuse: national survey findings. *Journal of Studies on Alcohol*, 58 (3), 264–71.

37 Burden, E. (2019) Trans sex attacker sent to female hostel. *The Times*, 27 February. Available at: https://www.thetimes.co.uk/article/trans -sex-attacker-sent-to-female-hostel-c3vw35c06

38 Manning, S. and Bindel, J. (2019) When he was a man called Mark he was locked up after threatening to kill the mother of his child. *Mail on Sunday*, 6 April.

39 Brean, J. (2018) Forced to share a room with transgender woman in Toronto shelter, sex abuse victim files human rights complaint. *National Post*, 2 August 2018.

40 BBC (2015) 'We just need to pee' transgender protest. 14 March. Available at: https://www.bbc.co.uk/news/blogs-trending-31860346

41 Bagagli, B.P., Chaves, V.C. and Zoppi Fontana, M.G. (2021) Trans women and public restrooms: the legal discourse and its violence. *Frontiers in Sociology*, 6, 652777.

42 British Standard, BS 6465 Part 1 on Sanitary Installations sets out the levels of provision required for female/male facilities. Kelly, L. (2016) 'The conducive context of violence against women and girls'. *Discover Society*, Issue 30.

43 The Workplace (Health, Safety and Welfare) Regulations 1992 state under Regulation 20 that employers need to provide separate rooms containing toilets for women and men.

44 S6465 Part 1, p. 19, Table 6 sets 'Minimum Sanitary Provision for Schools'. 2012 School Premises Regulations requires separate facilities for boys and girls over the age of 8.

45 Paragraph 2.1.2 of the UNICEF document on applying the UN Sustainable Development Goals to sanitation specifies that separate school toilets should be provided (SDG 6); Albuquerque, C. and Roaf, V. (2012) United Nations Report on The Human Right to Safe Drinking Water and Sanitation, pp. 35, 153–4.

46 https://blogs.worldbank.org/water/lack-access-toilet-and-handwas hing-materials-hits-women-and-girls-hardest-especially-when

47 Saleem, M., Burdett, T. and Heaslip, V. (2019) Health and social

impacts of open defecation on women: a systematic review. *BMC Public Health*, 19(1), 158.

48 Ibid.

49 McCann, D. (2021) Schoolgirls rejecting mixed toilets over boys' bad behaviour. *The Times*, 26 November. Available at: https://www.thetim es.co.uk/article/schoolgirls-rejecting-mixed-toilets-over-boys-bad-be haviour-vcgcrlxv5

50 EVAW (n.d.) We're facing a national crisis of sexual violence and harassment at school. The government and schools must take action now. Available at https://www.endviolenceagainstwomen.org.uk/campaign /metoo-at-school/

51 Gilligan, A. (2018) Unisex changing rooms put women in danger. *The Times*, 2 September. Available at: https://www.thetimes.co.uk/artic le/unisex-changing-rooms-put-women-in-danger-8lwbp8kgk#:~:text =Unisex%20changing%20rooms%20are%20more,less%20than%20half %20the%20total.

52 Ghate, S. (2019) Gender-bias in public bathroom designs. Medium, 1 August 2019. Available at: https://medium.com/@sepideghate/gender -bias-in-public-bathroom-designs-c72d2a38660c

53 Criado Perez, C. (2020) *Invisible Women*. London: Chatto and Windus, pp. 47–9.

54 BBC (2015) 'We just need to pee' transgender protest. 14 March. Available at: https://www.bbc.co.uk/news/blogs-trending-31860346

55 NHS (2019) Delivering same sex accommodation. Available at: https:// www.england.nhs.uk/statistics/wp-content/uploads/sites/2/2021/05 /NEW-Delivering_same_sex_accommodation_sep2019.pdf

56 Eaton, L. (2010) Experts doubt that NHS can scrap mixed sex wards by end of year. *BMJ*, 2010, 341, c4533. Available at https://www.bmj.com /content/341/bmj.c4533

57 Kentish, B. (2017) Soaring numbers of NHS patients forced to sleep alongside members of the opposite sex. *The Independent*, 20 November. Available at https://www.independent.co.uk/news/health/nhs-hospita ls-mixed-sex-wards-patients-soars-jeremy-hunt-philip-hammond-au tumn-budget-2017-a8064181.html

58 McLaughlin, M. (2020) NHS Greater Glasgow and Clyde withdraws trans advice for female-only wards. *The Times*, 28 December. Available at: https://www.thetimes.co.uk/article/nhs-greater-glasgow-and-clyde -withdraws-trans-advice-for-female-only-wards-5xmgxndd6

59 North, J. (2022) Hospital says patient could not have been raped because alleged attacker was transgender. *Scottish Daily Express*, 19 March. Available at https://www.scottishdailyexpress.co.uk/news/poli tics/hospital-says-patient-could-not-26506744

60 Bruni, F. (1996) Woman, 29, still in 10-year coma, is pregnant by a

rapist. *New York Times*, 25 January. Available at: https://www.nytimes
.com/1996/01/25/nyregion/woman-29-still-in-10-year-coma-is-preg
nant-by-a-rapist.html

61 El Ancasti (2015) Abusaron a una joven y la embarazaron estando en coma. 24 April. Available at: https://www.elancasti.com.ar/policiales /2015/4/24/abusaron-joven-embarazaron-estando-coma-257796.html

62 BBC (2022) Blackpool Victoria Hospital: Man in court over sex assault charges. 4 January. Available at: https://www.bbc.co.uk/ news/uk-england-lancashire-59869029

63 Murphy, S. (2020) GP who sexually assaulted 24 patients jailed for life. *The Guardian*, 7 February. Available at: https://www.theguardian.com /uk-news/2020/feb/07/gp-manish-shah-sexually-assaulted-24-patien ts-given-three-life-sentences

64 Norder, L. (n.d.) 5 doctors who abused patients while sedated. *The Atlanta Journal-Constitution*. Available at https://doctors.ajc.com/doc tor_sex_abuse_sedated/

65 BBC (2022) Paul Grayson: Voyeur Sheffield nurse who filmed up patients' gowns jailed. 10 May. Available at: https://www.bbc.co.uk/ne ws/uk-england-south-yorkshire-61396018

66 BBC (2021) Nursing assistant guilty of assaulting Crosshouse Hospital patients. 21 December. Available at: https://www.bbc.co.uk/news/uk -scotland-glasgow-west-59742641

67 Pearson-Jones, B. (2020) Witness who helped convict Dr Harold Shipman after he murdered one of her neighbours speaks publicly for the first time – and reveals she gave the serial killer a key to his victim's home where they found her body together. *Daily Mail*, 11 March. Available at: https://www.dailymail.co.uk/femail/article-8099343/Ha rold-Shipman-witness-breaks-silence-22-years-reveals-discovered-fri ends-body.html

68 Wallis, C.J.D., Jerath, A., Coburn, N., et al. (2022) Association of surgeon-patient sex concordance with postoperative outcomes. *JAMA Surgery*, 157 (2), 146–56.

69 Norder, 5 doctors who abused patients while sedated.

70 AbuDagga, A., Wolfe, S.M., Carome, M. and Oshel, R.E. (2019) Crossing the line: sexual misconduct by nurses reported to the National Practitioner Data Bank. *Public Health Nursing*, 36 (2), 109–17.

71 Chiarella, M. and Adrian, A. (2014) Boundary violations, gender and the nature of nursing work. *Nursing Ethics*, 21 (3), 267–77.

72 Zhong, E.H., McCarthy, C. and Alexander, M. (2016) A review of criminal convictions among nurses 2012–2013. *Journal of Nursing Regulation*, 7 (1), 27–33.

73 Unwin, E., Woolf, K., Wadlow, C., et al. (2015) Sex differences in med-ico-legal action against doctors: a systematic review and meta-analysis. *BMC Medicine*, 13, 172.

74 Smiley, R.A. and McCarthy, C. (2016) A mixed-methods study of gender differences in nurse reporting and nurse discipline. *Journal of Nursing Regulation*, 7 (3), 33–40.

75 Dhejne, C., Lichtenstein, P., Boman, M., et al. (2011) Long-term follow-up of transsexual persons undergoing sex reassignment surgery: cohort study in Sweden. *PLoS ONE*, 6(2), e16885.

76 Illawara Women's Health Centre. https://womenshealthcentre.com.au/he

77 Illawara Women's Health Centre. About us: https://womenshealthcentre.com.au/about-us/

78 Tuohy, W. (2021) Australia's first women-only mental health hospital will tackle soaring rates of illness. *The Age*, 13 July. Available at: https://www.theage.com.au/national/victoria/australia-s-first-women-only-mental-health-hospital-will-tackle-soaring-rates-of-illness-2021 0712-p588xp.html

79 Sardinha, H., Maheu-Giroux, M., Stockl, H, Meyer, S.R. and Garcia-Moreno, C. (2022) Global, regional, and national prevalence estimates of physical or sexual, or both, intimate partner violence against women in 2018. *The Lancet*, 399 (10327), 803–13.

80 Smith, S.G. and Breiding, M.J. (2011) Chronic disease and health behaviours linked to experiences of non-consensual sex among women and men. *Public Health*, 125 (9), 653–9.

81 Stein, M. and Barrett-Connor, E. (2000) Sexual assault and physical health: findings from a population-based study of older adults. *Psychosomatic Medicine*, 62 (6), 838–43.

82 Royal College of Obstetricians and Gynaecologists (2017) Available at: https://www.rcog.org.uk/blog

83 Bannerman, L. (2018) Smear test campaign drops the word 'woman' to avoid transgender offence. *The Times*, 15 June. Available at: https://www.thetimes.co.uk/article/smear-test-campaign-drops-the-word-woman-to-avoid-transgender-offence-263mj7f6s

84 Twitter (2020) @Tampax, 25 September. Available at: https://twitter.com/Tampax/status/1305952342504767491?s=20&t=38qv1UoRdYb MiTXsTb1eRg

85 Elmhirst, S. (2020) Tampon wars: the battle to overthrow the Tampax empire. *The Guardian*, 11 February. Available at: https://www.theguardian.com/society/2020/feb/11/tampon-wars-the-battle-to-overthrow-the-tampax-empire

86 Bloody Good Period (n.d.) We fight for menstrual equity and the rights of all people who bleed. Available at: https://www.bloodygoodperiod.com/

87 Bloody Good Period (n.d.) Mind Your Bloody Language. Available at: https://www.bloodygoodperiod.com/bloodylanguage

88 Bergdorf, M. (2018) Women are getting feminism wrong. *Grazia*, 27

February. Available at: https://graziadaily.co.uk/life/opinion/munroe-bergdorf-women-getting-feminism-wrong/

89 Ibid.

90 Bergdorf also criticised the ubiquitous pinkness of the pussy hats, pointing out that not all women have pink vulvas. This, I think, bears consideration. The originator of the idea for the hats was a woman of Korean heritage, Krista Suh, who describes herself as Asian-American. For Suh, pink was chosen because of the association with femininity, which she embraced saying 'It makes me sad and frustrated that somehow we associate whatever is the male association to be more dignified, to be taken more seriously. . . . It was important for me to go hard with pink and not veer away with that.' Pink is a colour stereotypically associated with girls of all ethnic backgrounds in the West and there is an argument to be made about reclaiming the colour or subverting the association and the pink being as much of an ironic comment as the reference to a pussy. However, I think those of us who are white or paler skinned women need to be careful about picking a symbol which unintentionally excludes women with darker skins. Whilst pussyhats in a range of colours would have had a different visual impact, and for Suh, creating a 'sea of pink' was important, a sea of hats of different shades could also have given a powerful message about unity across difference. Curry, K. (2020) Krista Suh inventor of the pussyhat, is all about pink. *Northwest Asian Weekly*, 12 March. Available at: https://nwasianweekly.com/2020/03/krista-suh-inventor-of-the-pussyhat-is-all-about-pink/

91 Dixon, H. (2021) Pregnancy charity defied trans activists. *Telegraph*, 8 October. Available at: https://www.telegraph.co.uk/news/2021/10/08/pregnancy-charity-defies-trans-activists-keeping-word-women/

92 British Pregnancy Advisory Service (2021) Our Values. Our Vision. Our Ambitions. Available at: https://www.bpas.org/media/3550/bpas-advocacy-values-vision-ambitions.pdf

93 Gribble, K.D., Bewley, S., Bartick, M.C., et al. (2022) Effective communication about pregnancy, birth, lactation, breastfeeding and newborn care: the importance of sexed language. *Frontiers in Global Women's Health*, 3, 818856.

94 Twitter. @piermorgan 31 July 2020. Available at https://twitter.com/piersmorgan/status/1289089410676543491?s=20&t=cGT9h-FFLcQtcm9oTq5oIg

95 Chantler-Hicks, L. (2020) Canterbury MP Rosie Duffield speaks out about threats received in wake of 'transphobe' Twitter row. Kent Online, 12 October 2020. Available at: https://www.kentonline.co.uk/canterbury/news/ive-received-threats-but-will-not-be-silenced-235405/

96 Twitter. @RosieDuffield1 1 August 2020. Available at: https://twitter

.com/RosieDuffield1/status/1289498350857977858?s=20&t=f1VIlsLI
DCzAcq-ROi8P9w

97 ITV (2021) Canterbury MP forced to stay away from Labour Party
    conference after extremist threats. 20 September. Available at: https://
    www.itv.com/news/meridian/2021-09-19/canterbury-mp-forced-to-
    stay-away-from-party-conference-after-extremist-threats

98 BBC (2021) Labour conference: Not right to say only women have a
    cervix, says Starmer. 26 September. Available at: https://www.bbc.co.uk
    /news/uk-politics-58698406

99 Twitter @EmilyThornberry 2022 Available at: twitter.com/Emily
    Thornberry/status/1553656918220177408

100 Steward, C. (2021) Labour Party should have done better on trans
    rights. *The Herald*, 31 October. Available at: https://www.heraldscotla
    nd.com/opinion/19617372.labour-party-done-better-trans-rights/

101 Wade, M. (2022) Student midwives at Napier University taught that
    men can get pregnant. *The Times*, 29 April. Available at: https://www.
    thetimes.co.uk/article/student-midwives-at-napier-university-taught-
    that-men-can-get-pregnant-bsxvj0dcp

102 Many of us do not wish to identify with a gender but instead see the
    solution as abolishing stereotypes. Gender identity ideology should not
    be enforced on those who do not uphold it.

103 Dahlen, S. (2020) De-sexing the medical record? An examination of sex
    versus gender identity in the General Medical Council's trans health-
    care ethical advice. *The New Bioethics*, 26 (1), 38–52.

104 García-Acosta, J.M., San Juan-Valdivia, R.M., Fernández-Martínez,
    A.D., Lorenzo-Rocha, N.D. and Castro-Peraza, M.E. (2020) Trans*
    pregnancy and lactation: a literature review from a nursing perspec-
    tive. *International Journal of Environmental Research and Public
    Health*, 17 (1), 44.

105 Chan, K.J., Liang, J.J., Jolly, D., Weinand, J.D. and Safer, J.D. (2018)
    Exogenous testosterone does not induce or exacerbate the metabolic
    features associated with PCOS among transgender men. *Endocrine
    Practice*, 24 (6), 565–72

106 Baba, T., Endo, T., Honma, H. and Kitajima, Y. (2007) Association
    between polycystic ovary syndrome and female-to-male transsexuality.
    Human Reproduction (Oxford, England), 22 (4), 1011–16.

107 Hurley, P. (2017) Ovarian cancer risk and incidence in transgender
    men. Available at: https://cancer-network.org/wp-content/uploads/20
    17/02/Trans_men_and_ovarian_cancer.pdf

108 Womensgrid archive (2012) RadFem 2012 is a women-only radical
    feminist conference and social event. Available at: http://www.women
    sgrid.org.uk/archive/2012/05/16/radfem-2012-is-a-women-only-radi
    cal-feminist-conference-and-social-event/

109 Kaveney, R. (2012) Radical feminists are acting like a cult. *The Guardian*,

25 May. Available at: https://www.theguardian.com/commentisfree/20 12/may/25/radical-feminism-trans-radfem2012

110   Jeffreys, S. (2012) Let us be free to debate transgenderism without being accused of 'hate speech'. *The Guardian*, 29 May. Available at: https://www.theguardian.com/commentisfree/2012/may/29/transgen derism-hate-speech

111   Monaghan, G. (2013) Radical feminists barred from London Irish venue. *The Times*, 21 April. Available at: https://www.thetimes.co.uk/ar ticle/radical-feminists-barred-from-london-irish-venue-pg8skjlg3gj

112   Burns, I. (2018) Millwall football club 'caves in to transgender activists and cancels feminists' meeting after threats'. *Daily Mail*, 11 March. Available at: https://www.dailymail.co.uk/news/article-5487525/Tou gh-Millwall-football-club-caves-transgender-activists.html

113   SWERF stands for 'sex worker exclusionary radical feminist', following the TERF acronym, and is used by some sex trade advocates against sex trade abolitionists. It is logically nonsensical. Feminists who resist the sex trade do not exclude or denigrate the women who are exploited; in fact many abolitionist activists are women who have survived and exited prostitution.

114   Murphy, M. (2017) Vancouver Women's Library opens amid anti-feminist backlash. Available at: https://www.feministcurrent.com/20 17/02/07/vancouver-womens-library-opens-amid-anti-feminist-back lash/

115   Bannerman, L. (2018) Trans attacker is a thug, says feminist. *The Times*, 12 April. Available at: https://www.thetimes.co.uk/ article/trans-attacker-tara-wolf-is-a-thug-says-feminist-maria-maclachlan-pq0bwvthv

116   Pearson-Jones, B. (2018) Transgender model who punched feminist and smashed her £120 camera in violent brawl at Hyde Park Speakers' Corner protest walks free from court. *Daily Mail*, 13 April. Available at: https://www.dailymail.co.uk/news/article-5613057/Model-punch ed-feminist-smashed-120-camera-violent-brawl-walks-free-court .html

117   CathyBrennan@towntatle (2021) Twitter: 'I called her a TERF cunt, which is what she is. I'm a trans person, so the mere fact of my exist-ence is terrifying to her lol. I did not attempt to assault her', 4:40 PM, 6 August 2021.

118   Davison, G. (2019) Feminist speaker Julie Bindel 'attacked by transgen-der person' at Edinburgh University after talk. *The Scotsman*, 6 June. Available at: https://www.scotsman.com/news/scottish-news/feminist -speaker-julie-bindel-attacked-transgender-person-edinburgh-univer sity-after-talk-545841

119   UN Women (2020) Visualising the data: women's representation in society. Available at: https://www.unwomen.org/en/digital-library/

multimedia/2020/2/infographic-visualizing-the-data-womens-repre
sentation

120 Linda Wertmuller, *Seven Beauties* (1975); Jane Campion, *The Piano*
(1993); Sofia Coppola, *Lost in Translation* (2003); Kathryn Bigelow, *The
Hurt Locker* (2009); Greta Gerwig, *Lady Bird* (2017); Emerald Fennell,
Promising Young Woman (2020); Chloe Zhoa, *Nomadland* (2021), Jane
Campion, *The Power of the Dog* (2022).

121 UN Women (2020) Visualizing the data: Women's representation in
society.

122 Madaan, N. (2018) Judging a book by its description: analysing gender
stereotypes in the Man Bookers prize winning fiction. Available at:
https://deepai.org/publication/judging-a-book-by-its-description-ana
lysing-gender-stereotypes-in-the-man-bookers-prize-winning-fiction

123 Bannerman, L. (2018) Anger over women's business honour for cross-
dressing banker. *The Times*, 22 September. Available at: https://www
.thetimes.co.uk/article/anger-over-women-s-business-honour-for-cro
ss-dressing-banker-h0gv3l7nw

124 BBC (2015) Caitlyn Jenner makes Woman's Hour Power List. 1 July.
Available at: https://www.bbc.co.uk/news/entertainment-arts-3334
4317

125 Harris, K., Jefferson, W. and Scott, S. (2015) Caitlyn Jenner on the
moment she felt most proud to be a woman in 2015. Buzzfeed, 10
November. Available at: https://www.buzzfeed.com/kristinharris/cait
lyn-jenner-the-power-of-the-woman-hasnt-been-unleashed

126 Cain, S. (2021) Women's prize condemns online attack on trans nomi-
nee Torrey Peters. *The Guardian*, 7 April. Available at: https://www.th
eguardian.com/books/2021/apr/07/womens-prize-condemns-online
-attack-on-trans-nominee-torrey-peters-detransition-baby

127 Old Square Chambers (2022) Robin White shortlisted for an award at
the Women, Influence & Power in Law UK Awards 2022. 24 January.
Available at: https://oldsquare.co.uk/robin-white-shortlisted-for-awa
rd-at-the-women-influence-power-in-law-uk-awards-2022/

128 https://revistamarieclaire.globo.com/Feminismo/noticia/2021/12/se
te-mulheres-que-fizeram-diferenca-pelos-direitos-humanos-no-brasil
.html

129 Shaw, D. (2019) 'Transgender' politician expelled from party, accused
of sexual exploitation of minors, property coup. Updated 8 January
2022. Available at: https://www.womenarehuman.com/transgender
-politician-expelled-from-party-amidst-accusations-of-sexual-exploi
tation-of-minors-indianara-siqueira/

130 Miller, L. (2014) The Trans-Everything CEO. *New York Mag*, 7
September. Available at: https://nymag.com/news/features/martine
-rothblatt-transgender-ceo/

131 Bindel, J. (2020) Triumph of the trans lobbyists. The Critic, 20 January.

Available at: https://thecritic.co.uk/issues/january-2020/triumph-of
-the-trans-lobbyists/

132 New York Times (2020) World Rugby bars transgender women, baf-
fling players. Available at: https://www.nytimes.com/2020/10/26/spor
ts/olympics/world-rugby-transgender-women.html

133 England Rugby (2019) Policy for the participation of transgender
& non-binary gender players. Available at: https://www.englandrug
by.com/dxdam/26/26de38f3-d82f-4816-8be3-b582f6a9f757/Transgen
derPolicy.pdf

134 Ingle, S. (2021) Trans women in English rugby could face height and
weight safety checks. *The Guardian*, 30 March. Available at: https://
www.theguardian.com/sport/2021/mar/30/trans-women-in-english
-rugby-could-face-height-and-weight-safety-checks

135 Reza, R. (2019) Transgender cyclist Rachel McKinnon wins second-
straight World Masters Title. Bicycling, 24 October. Available at:
https://www.bicycling.com/news/a29578581/rachel-mckinnon-world
-championship-masters-win-transgender-sport-debate/

136 BBC (2021) Laurel Hubbard: The reluctant history-maker at the centre
of sport's transgender debate. 1 August. Available at: https://www.bbc
.co.uk/sport/olympics/57989022

137 Reilly, P. (2022) Teammates say they are uncomfortable changing in
locker room with trans UPenn swimmer Lia Thomas. *New York Post*, 27
January. Available at: https://nypost.com/2022/01/27/teammates-are
-uneasy-changing-in-locker-room-with-trans-upenn-swimmer-lia-th
omas/

138 Sanchez, R. (2022) 'I am Lia': The trans swimmer dividing America tells
her story. SI, 3 March. Available at: https://www.si.com/college/2022
/03/03/lia-thomas-penn-swimmer-transgender-woman-daily-cover

139 Allen, K. (2018) Transgender teens outrun track and field competitors
but critics close behind. ABC News, 13 June. Available at: https://abcn
ews.go.com/US/transgender-teens-outrun-track-field-competitors-cri
tics-close/story?id=55856294

140 The Boardr (2022) The Boardr Open at New York City women's finals
presented by DC results. 25 June. Available at: https://theboardr.com
/results/9288/The-Boardr-Open-at-New-York-City-Womens-FINALS
-Presented-by-DC

141 Smith, J. (2022) Trans skateboarder, 29, who beat 13-year-old girl to
first prize in women's competition. *Daily Mail*, 27 June. Available at:
https://www.dailymail.co.uk/news/article-10958359/Trans-skateboar
der-claimed-prize-girl-13-divorced-ex-Navy-dad-three.html

142 Ibid.

143 Silverman, T. (2022) Instagram post, 17 May. Available at: https://www.
instagram.com/p/CdqeekVMFBo/

144 Gupta, S. (2016) The group of muscles in the abdominal region, the

obliques and part of the back, play a pivotal role in skateboarding performance. Redbull, 19 October. Available at: https://www.redbull.com/in-en/core-muscles-used-in-skateboarding.

145 Pool, T. (2022) Twitter. https://twitter.com/Timcast/status/152699646 5431859202?s=20&t=fRBoHYuRLkpmUE2mMt_XyQ

146 WPUK (2019) A woman's place is on the podium. 12 July. Available at: https://womansplaceuk.org/2019/07/12/a-womans-place-is-on-the -podium/

147 Hilton, E. (2019) Speech at Woman's Place UK, A woman's place is on the podium. Available at: https://www.youtube.com/watch?v=pzg9Qt QelR8

148 Roberts, T.A., Smalley, J. and Ahrendt, D. (2021) Effect of gender affirming hormones on athletic performance in transwomen and transmen: implications for sporting organisations and legislators. *British Journal of Sports Medicine*, 55 (11).

149 Hilton, E.N. and Lundberg, T.R. (2021) Transgender women in the female category of sport: perspectives on testosterone suppression and performance advantage. *Sports Medicine*, 51, 199–214.

150 Devine, C. (2022) Female Olympians' voices: Female sports categories and International Olympic Committee Transgender guidelines. *International Review for the Sociology of Sport*, 57 (3), 335–61.

151 Urbanski, D. (2019) HS girl swimmer near tears after transgenders get 'unrestricted' access to locker room where she changes 'multiple times, naked' in front of others. Blaze media, 20 November. Available at: https://www.theblaze.com/news/hs-girl-near-tears-after-transgenders -get-unrestricted-access-to-locker-room

152 Watts, H. (2020) Girlguiding: campfires, crafts and compelled belief. Woman's Place UK. Available at: https://womansplaceuk.org/2020/07 /08/girlguiding-campfires-crafts-compelled-belief/

153 Corless, B. (2022) Girlguiding should describe itself as mixed not single-sex as it welcomes trans members, says former leader. *The Telegraph*, 22 April. Available at: https://www.telegraph.co.uk/news /2022/04/24/girlguiding-should-describe-mixed-not-single-sex-welco mes-trans/

154 Red Flag Walks (2019) 'We're not ugly, we're not beautiful – we're angry!': The protest by feminists at the Miss World contest, 20th November 1970. Available at: https://redflagwalks.wordpress.com/20 19/07/22/were-not-ugly-were-not-beautiful-were-angry-the-protest -by-feminists-at-the-miss-world-contest-20th-november-1970/

155 Short, C. (2005) *An Honourable Deception? New Labour, Iraq, and the Misuse of Power*. London: Simon and Schuster.

156 Glozer, C. and McCarthy, L. (2021) No More Page 3: how a feminist collective took on a media behemoth to challenge everyday sexism.

Available at: https://theconversation.com/no-more-page-3-how-a-feminist-collective-took-on-a-media-behemoth-to-challenge-every day-sexism-156478

157   Gander, K. (2015) The Sun drops page 3? No More Page Three hails 'historic moment' amid reports tabloid newspaper has cancelled topless models. *The Independent*, 20 January. Available at: https://www.independent.co.uk/news/media/press/topless-models-on-page-three-dropped-9988831.html

158   Berger, J. (2008 [1972]) *Ways of Seeing*. London: Penguin, p. 47.

159   Mulvey, L. (1989) Visual pleasure and narrative cinema. In *Visual and Other Pleasures*. London: Palgrave Macmillan.

160   Kruti Walsh (2022) personal correspondence

161   Johnson, R. (2012) The power of her sex. Available at: https://www.patheos.com/blogs/afewgrownmen/2012/08/the-power-of-her-sex/

162   Lees, P. (2014) I love wolf-whistles and catcalls – am I a bad feminist? Vice, 5 March. Available at: https://www.vice.com/en/article/gq8v93/i-love-wolf-whistles-and-catcalls-am-i-a-bad-feminist

163   Bloom, L. (2021) Twitter. Available at: https://twitter.com/leynabloom/status/1417134760506413060?s=20&t=0rjQJ5FL5HUo5X1UG8ekGA

164   Lavery, G. (2019) Comme une femme: on returning to France post-transition. Them, 17 June. Available at: https://www.them.us/story/returning-to-france-post-transition

165   National Centre for Lesbian Rights. https://www.nclrights.org/our-work/youth/transgender-youth/

166   Denholm, M. (2021) Bid to exclude 'people with penises' from lesbian events 'unlawful'. The Australian, 18 July. Available at: https://amp.theaustralian.com.au/nation/bid-to-exclude-people-with-penises-from-lesbian-events-unlawful/news-story/31b6a5e8c1a91569536343750bd942c5

167   Hoyle, J. (2022) My cause: High Court Challenge. Available at: https://www.mycause.com.au/p/287142/high-court-challenge?popup=1

168   Petter, O. (2021) Kathleen Stock: Ex-Sussex professor says there's 'real pressure' to accept trans women can be lesbians. *The Independent*, 3 November. Available at: https://www.independent.co.uk/life-style/women/kathleen-stock-trans-bbc-womens-hour-b1950484.html

169   Morgan, C. (2021) Lesbian barrister, 43, claims she sees 'sinister' men claiming to be trans women 'bully naïve and vulnerable' lesbian girls as young as 14 into sex. MailOnline, 27 October. Available at: https://www.dailymail.co.uk/femail/article-10132549/Lesbian-claims-shes-seen-people-identify-trans-women-bully-young-girls-relationship.html

170   Bartosch, J. (2021) Trans lobby group Stonewall brands lesbians 'sexual racists' for raising concerns about being pressured into having sex with transgender women who still have male genitals. MailOnline, 20

November. Available at: https://www.dailymail.co.uk/news/article-102
25111/Stonewall-brands-lesbians-sexual-racists-raising-concerns-sex
-transgender-women.html
171 Parker, J. and Lawrie, E. (2021) Stonewall boss defends new strategy
amid criticism. BBC, 29 May. Available at: https://www.bbc.co.uk/ne
ws/uk-57281448
172 Carmo, R., Grams, A. and Magalhães, T. (2011) Men as victims of intimate partner violence. *Journal of Forensic and Legal Medicine*, 18 (8),
355–9.
173 Turell, S.C. (1999) Seeking help for same-sex relationship abuses.
Journal of Gay & Lesbian Social Services, 10 (2), 35–49.

Chapter 6: Sisters are Doing it for Themselves
1 Whilst acknowledging that some organisations may choose to or be
pressured to include males with transgender identities in women's
services.
2 Sex Matters (2022) Karen Ingala Smith talks about single-sex services.
Available at: https://sex-matters.org/posts/updates/karen-ingala-smith
-talks-about-single-sex-services/
3 Gilligan, A. (2018) Women's refuges may get transgender staff. *The
Sunday Times*, 4 February. Available at: https://thetimes.co.uk/article/
womens-refuges-may-get-transgender-staff-3txhcr8mb
4 Women's Aid (2021) Written evidence submitted by the Women's Aid
Federation of England. Available at: https://publications.parliament.uk
/pa/cm5801/cmpublic/DomesticAbuse/memo/DAB65.pdf
5 Women's Aid (2022) Single sex services statement. Available at: https://
www.womensaid.org.uk/womens-aid-single-sex-services-statement/
6 Twitter: @ForWomenscot 4 April 2022: 'It is of note that @womens-
aid reached these sensible conclusions after a year-long consultation
of members and stakeholders. @scotwomensaid has so far failed to
do likewise: the policy is dictated from the Gov funded umbrella org.'
Available at https://twitter.com/ForWomenScot/status/1510885678900
523010?s=20&t=8gHDmfePVeIMXIIdv4WCOA
7 Twitter: @ForWomenscot 4 April 2022: Yes, and many centres do not
agree with / conform to this policy. But women don't realise and it is
deterring victims. Available at: https://twitter.com/ForWomenScot/sta
tus/1510888416988340228?s=20&t=8gHDmfePVeIMXIIdv4WCOA
8 Women's Resource Centre (2022) WRC Statement on women-only
services and sex-based rights. Available at: https://www.wrc.org.uk/
blog/wrc-statement-on-women-only-services-and-sex-based-rights
9 For example, Women's Resource Centre (2006) Why women? Available

at: https://www.wrc.org.uk/Handlers/Download.ashx?IDMF=dffb1f5e-
aa65-4f01-8f03-ca5d4bd30170

10 Smethers, S. (2020) Sex and gender identity: finding a way forward.
    Fawcett Society. Available at: https://www.fawcettsociety.org.uk/blog/
    sex-and-gender-identity-finding-a-way-forward

11 =Shakti Women's Aid (2008-2017), Rape Crisis Scotland (2014 - 2018),
    Forth Valley Rape Crisis Centre(2018 - 2021). LinkedIn, https://
    uk.linkedin.com/in/mridul-wadhwa

12 =YouTube. My Genderation (2019) Trans And: Mridul. Transgender
    Stories. 23 May. Available at: https://youtu.be/HT_ryngVhcU

13 Wadhwa, M. (2021) Welcome to Mridul Wadhwa, our new CEO. Available
    at: https://www.ercc.scot/welcome-to-mridul-wadhwa-our-new-ceo/

14 Guilty Feminist – 265. Creating Our Own World with Kemah Bob and
    Mridul Wadhwa. Transcribed by FOR Women Scotland. Available at:
    https://forwomen.scot/wp-content/uploads/2021/08/Mridul-Wadhwa
    -Guilty-Feminist-transcript.pdf

15 Mridul Wadhwa (2021) Speaking at SayiT Sheffield. Transcript by Jean
    Hatchet. Available at https://www.jeanhatchet.com/post/mridul-wadh
    wa-speaking-at-sayit-sheffield-transcript

16 van der Kolk, *The Body Keeps the Score*, p. 210.

17 Learmonth, A. (2020) MSPs overwhelmingly vote to replace gender
    with sex in rape support law. The National, 10 December. Available at:
    thenatiuonal.scot/news/18936441.msps-overwhelmingly-vot-to-teplace-
    gender-rape-sex-law/

18 Twitter (2021) @mridul_wadhwa 'My GP told me the other day to eat
    more greens. So I have just gone and become one.' 4.42pm 18 December.
    Since deleted.

19 Alan Fleming, a former police officer, has been CEO of Birmingham
    Crisis Centre since 2006 and The Sligo Rape Crisis and Counselling
    Centre in Ireland has had a male CEO, David Madden, since 2019.

20 Usually less than half to one per cent of the people using our services
    every year are male, in numerical terms around ten a year.

21 For example, Transactual's website states 'trans women are entitled
    to be treated the same as any other woman and to access women-only
    spaces. Under the law, exceptions to this may be applied on a case-by-
    case basis if it is shown to be proportionate and justifiable to do so. The
    legal bar for what is proportionate and justifiable is set very high and
    is rarely challenged. For example, if a trans woman had a history of
    sexually harassing other women, it may be justifiable and proportionate
    to deny her membership of a women-only society and the application

of the exception under the law would be legal. However, if the same women-only society banned all trans women, it would be a breach of the Equality Act (2010) because the decision would not be proportionate, justifiable or taken on a case-by-case basis.' This is not a correct interpretation of the law. Available at https://www.transactual.org.uk/equality-act

22 FOVAS (Female-Only, Violence and Abuse Survivors) (2018) Open letter to UK Women's Organisations from female survivors of male violence. Available at https://fovas.wordpress.com/

23 https://womansplaceuk.org/

24 FPFW (2018) Supporting Women in Domestic and Sexual Violence Services. Available at: https://fairplayforwomen.com/wp-content/uploads/2018/09/FPFW_report_19SEPT2018.pdf

25 Richards, A. (2018) Female campaigners 'self-identify' as men to infiltrate male-only pool at Hampstead Heath. *Evening Standard*, 29 May. Available at: https://www.standard.co.uk/news/uk/female-campaigners-selfidentify-as-men-to-infiltrate-male-only-pool-at-hampstead-heath-a3850556.html

26 Get the L Out UK: https://www.gettheloutuk.com/

27 Keep Prisons Single Sex: https://kpssinfo.org/

28 Sex Matters: https://sex-matters.org/

29 Frontline Feminists Scotland: https://www.frontlinefeministsscotland.com/

30 Raúf, O. (2019) The sheer audacity of our existence. Available at: https://womansplaceuk.org/2019/10/01/the-sheer-audacity-of-our-existence/

31 Freitas, C. (2020) Solidarity in action: Cátia Freitas. Available at: https://womansplaceuk.org/2020/02/18/solidarity-in-action-catia-freitas/

32 Smith, J. (2022) Has Sadiq Khan sacrificed women? Unherd, 25 February. Available at: https://unherd.com/2022/02/has-sadiq-khan-sacrificed-women/

33 Rowling, J.K. (2020) J.K. Rowling writes about her reasons for speaking out on sex and gender issues. Available at: https://www.jkrowling.com/opinions/j-k-rowling-writes-about-her-reasons-for-speaking-out-on-sex-and-gender-issues/

34 Rouse, S. (2021) JK Rowling receives 'hundreds of rape and assassination threats' after airing gender views. *Express*, 20 July. Available at: https://www.express.co.uk/celebrity-news/1464916/JK-Rowling-pipe-bomb-death-threat-trans-gender-Harry-Potter-twitter-news-latest-update

Chapter 7: 'Trans Rights are Human Rights'

1 Biggs, M. (2022) Queer theory and the transition from sex to gender in English prisons. *Journal of Controversial Ideas*, 2 (1), 2.

2 United Nations (1948) Universal Declaration of Human Rights. Available at: https://www.un.org/en/about-us/universal-declaration-of-human-rights

3 Self-identification would allow people to change their legally recognised 'gender', including on key official documents like birth certificates or passports, without going through a verification process. It was one of the proposals being considered under reform of the Gender Recognition Act. Although it was announced in September 2020, the proposal was scrapped, the government agreed to cut the cost of applying for a Gender Recognition Certificate. Liz Truss (2020) Statement – Response to GRA(2004) consultation. Available at: https://questions-statements.parliament.uk/written-statements/detail/2020-09-22/hcws462

4 Joyce, H. (2021) *Trans*. London: One World, p. 265.

5 Pidd, H. (2017) Transgender woman at male prison did not mean to kill herself, jury finds. *The Guardian*, 19 May. Available at: https://www.theguardian.com/uk-news/2017/may/19/jury-returns-verdict-on-transgender-woman-found-dead-in-male-prison

6 Worley, W. (2019) Transgender woman 'raped 2,000 times' in all-male prison. *The Independent*, 7 August. Available at: https://www.independent.co.uk/news/world/australasia/transgender-woman-raped-2-000-times-male-prison-a6989366.html

7 Neus, N. (2021) Trans women are still incarcerated with men and it's putting their lives at risk. CNN, 23 June. Available at: https://edition.cnn.com/2021/06/23/us/trans-women-incarceration/index.html

8 Inquest (2018) Still dying on the inside. Available at: https://barrowcadbury.org.uk/wp-content/uploads/2018/10/Still_Dying_on_the_Inside_2_May_2018_INQUEST.pdf, p. 13.

9 Article 2 of the HRA: 'Everyone's right to life shall be protected by law'. Article 3 protects: the right to freedom from torture and inhuman and degrading treatment.

10 London Assembly Health Committee (2022) Trans health matters: improving access to healthcare for trans and gender-diverse Londoners. Available at: https://www.london.gov.uk/press-releases/assembly/transgender-people-failed-by-lack-of-nhs-data-0

11 Simmons-Duffin, S. (2020) Transgender health protections reversed by Trump Administration. NPR, 12 June. Available at: https://www.npr.org/sections/health-shots/2020/06/12/868073068/transgender-

health-protections-reversed-by-trump-administration?t=16532232942
31

12 Kerr, L., Fisher, C. and Jones, T. (2019) TRANScending discrimination
in health & cancer care: a study of trans & gender diverse Australians
(ARCSHS Monograph Series No. 117). Bundoora: Australian Research
Centre in Sex, Health & Society, La Trobe.

13 Universal Declaration of Human Rights, Article 25.

14 Waterson, J. (2020) Trans activists write to Sun condemning JK Rowling
abuse story. *The Guardian*, 15 June. Available at: https://www.theguar
dian.com/books/2020/jun/15/trans-and-non-binary-activists-write-to
-sun-in-support-of-jk-rowling

15 O'Hara, M.E. (2017) Trump pulls back Obama-era protections for
women workers. NBC News, 3 April. Available at: https://www.nbcn
ews.com/news/us-news/trump-pulls-back-obama-era-protections-
women-workers-n741041

16 Lambada Legal (2017) What did Obama do for transgender students and
how did Trump take it away? Available at: https://www.lambdalegal.org
/blog/20170225_trans-students-faq

17 Vagianos, A. (2018) The Violence Against Women Act Just Expired.
Huffpost, 27 December. Available at: https://www.huffingtonpost.co.uk
/entry/the-violence-against-women-act-just-expired_n_5c24d8aae4b05
c88b6fe046e

18 Dorf-Kamienny, S. (2019) How Trump's Anti-Immigration Policies are
Hurting Domestic Violence Survivors. Ms, 25 June. Available at: https://
msmagazine.com/2019/06/25/how-trumps-anti-immigration-policies
-are-hurting-domestic-violence-survivors/

19 Democracy Now (2019) 'A shameful week for the US': Trump Admin
guts UN Resolution to end rape as weapon of war. 26 April. Available
at: https://www.democracynow.org/2019/4/26/a_shameful_week_for_
the_us

20 Scott, D. (2021) The Trump presidency is over, and Obamacare is still
alive. Vox, 19 January. Available at: https://www.vox.com/policy-and-po
litics/22238505/donald-trump-obamacare-joe-biden

21 Macias, A. (2021) Biden reverses Trump's ban on transgender people
enlisting in the military. CNBC, 25 January. Available at: https://www
.cnbc.com/2021/01/25/biden-reverses-trumps-ban-on-transgender-
people-enlisting-in-the-military.html

22 The White House (2021) Executive Order on Improving Public Safety
and Criminal Justice for Native Americans and Addressing the Crisis
of Missing or Murdered Indigenous People. 15 November. Available at:

https://www.whitehouse.gov/briefing-room/presidential-actions/2021
/11/15/executive-order-on-improving-public-safety-and-criminal-jus
tice-for-native-americans-and-addressing-the-crisis-of-missing-or-mur
dered-indigenous-people/

23 BBC (2022) Ketanji Brown Jackson 'means the world' to every black
girl. BBC, 8 April. Available at: https://www.bbc.co.uk/news/world-us-
canada-61018765

24 Gerstein, J. and Ward, A. (2022) Supreme Court has voted to overturn abortion rights, draft opinion shows. Politico, 3 May. Available at:
https://www.politico.com/news/2022/05/02/supreme-court-abortion
-draft-opinion-00029473

25 Liptak, A. (2021) Supreme Court to hear abortion case challenging Roe
v. Wade. New York Times, 17 May, updated 3 May 2022. Available at:
https://www.nytimes.com/2021/05/17/us/politics/supreme-court-roe
-wade.html

26 Government Equalities Office (2016) Pre-Consultation Equality Impact
Assessment for the Gender Recognition Act 2004. Available at: https://
consult.education.gov.uk/government-equalities-office/reform-of-the-
gender-recognition-act/user_uploads/gra-psed-assessment.pdf

27 Stock, K. (2021) Material Girls: Why Reality Matters for Feminism.
London: Fleet, p. 213.

28 Government Equalities Office (2020) Gender Recognition Act: analysis
of consultation responses. Available at: https://assets.publishing.service
.gov.uk/government/uploads/system/uploads/attachment_data/file/91
9890/Analysis_of_responses_Gender_Recognition_Act.pdf

29 Dillon, S. (2021) Single sex services on a spectrum. Available at: https://
shonaghdillon.co.uk/single-sex-services-on-a-spectrum/

30 Stonewall (2015) Women and Equalities Select Committee Inquiry on
Transgender Equality. Available at: https://www.stonewall.org.uk/wo
men-and-equalities-select-committee-inquiry-transgender-equality

31 Gendered Intelligence (2015) Written evidence submitted by Gendered
Intelligence to the Transgender Equality Inquiry. Available at: http://
data.parliament.uk/writtenevidence/committeeevidence.svc/evidence
document/women-and-equalities-committee/transgender-equality/
written/19557.pdf

32 Scottish Transgender Alliance (2015) Written evidence submitted by
Scottish Transgender Alliance, Equality Network to the Transgender
Equality Inquiry. Available at: http://data.parliament.uk/writteneviden
ce/committeeevidence.svc/evidencedocument/women-and-equalities-
committee/transgender-equality/written/19659.pdf

33 Dentons Europe LLP (2019) Only adults? Good practices in legal gender recognition for youth. Available at: https://www.iglyo.com/wp-content/uploads/2019/11/IGLYO_v3-1.pdf

34 Reid, S. (2022) 'We are not inherently male or female': Stonewall campaigner sparks storm by saying bodies 'are just bodies' in discrimination case against charity. *MailOnline*, 11 May. Available at: https://www.dailymail.co.uk/news/article-10807211/We-not-inherently-male-female-Stonewall-campaigner-says-bodies-just-bodies.html

35 Stonewall. Ruth Hunt. Available at: https://www.stonewall.org.uk/people/ruth-hunt

36 The meeting was held on 30 August 2014. Stonewall. Available at: https://www.stonewall.org.uk/our-work/campaigns/2015-stonewall-extends-remit-become-lgbt-charity-and-begins-journey-trans

37 Stonewall. A Vision for Change. Available at: https://www.stonewall.org.uk/vision-change#:~:text='A%20Vision%20for%20Change'%20is,trans%20people%20across%20the%20UK.

38 Information from publicly available accounts accessed via Companies House. Available at https://find-and-update.company-information.service.gov.uk/company/02412299/filing-history?page=7

39 Stonewall. Diversity Champions Programme. Available at: https://www.stonewall.org.uk/diversity-champions-programme

40 Stonewall Annual Accounts for the 18-month period ending March 2021. Available at: https://find-and-update.company-information.service.gov.uk/company/02412299/filing-history/MzMyNTM4MTE2NGFkaXF6a2N4/document?format=pdf&download=0

41 Sex Matters. Stonewall Champions List. Available at: https://sex-matters.org/stonewall-champions-list/

42 See reference in chapter 5 to Nancy Kelly, CEO, Stonewall, likening lesbians' concerns about the cotton ceiling as being equivalent to 'sexual racism' and also comparing so-called 'gender-critical' beliefs to antisemitism.

43 Manning, S. (2020) Event dedicated to stopping violence against women is 'hijacked by trendy campaigns'. *Mail on Sunday*, 29 November. Available at https://www.dailymail.co.uk/news/article-8997413/Event-dedicated-stopping-violence-against-women-hijacked-trendy-campaigns.html

44 Skopeliti, C. (2020) Olivia Colman, Jameela Jamil and Paloma Faith condemn 'violence and hostility' against trans women in open letter. *The Independent*, 25 November. Available at: https://www.independent.co.uk/news/uk/home-news/olivia-colman-jameela-jamil-paloma-faith-trans-women-letter-b1761714.html

45 Manning, Event dedicated to stopping violence against women.
46 Claimsmaking happens when people attempt to describe a situation in a particular way and to have that understanding become widely accepted as a basis for action. For example, claiming that poor diets cause health problems for people on benefits rather than saying that social inequality and poverty lead to health inequalities.
47 Dillon, S. (2021) #TERF/Bigot/Transphobe' – 'We found the witch, burn her!' A contextual constructionist account of the silencing of feminist discourse on the proposed changes to the Gender Recognition Act 2004, and the policy capture of transgender ideology, focusing on the potential impacts and consequences for female-only spaces for victims of male violence. Doctoral thesis, University of Portsmouth.
48 Ibid.
49 Scottish National Party (SNP) MP for Lanark and Hamilton East and the SNP Shadow Attorney General.
50 Amy Griffiths was described by friends as a 'hero of the LGBT community': Bayliss, C. (2019) Transgender woman, 51, who was 'hero of LGBT community' is found murdered. Daily Mail, 18 January. Available at: https://www.dailymail.co.uk/news/article-6606949/Murdered-transgen der-woman-51-hero-LGBT-community.html
51 Stonewall. The Truth About Trans. Available at: https://www.stonewall .org.uk/sites/default/files/trans_stats.pdf
52 Mermaids (2019) Written evidence to Parliamentary Committee. Available at: https://committees.parliament.uk/writtenevidence/23299/pdf/
53 Strudwick, P. (2014) Nearly half of young transgender people have attempted suicide – UK survey. The Guardian, 19 November. Available at: https://www.theguardian.com/society/2014/nov/19/young-transgen der-suicide-attempts-survey
54 Government Equalities Office (2018) Reform of the GRA – Government Consultation. Available at: https://assets.publishing.service.gov.uk/gov ernment/uploads/system/uploads/attachment_data/file/721725/GRA-Consultation-document.pdf, pp. 2 and 10.
55 Nodin, N., Peel, E., Tyler, A. and Rivers, I. (2015) The RaRE Research Report. Available at: http://www.queerfutures.co.uk/wp-content/uploa ds/2015/04/RARE_Research_Report_PACE_2015.pdf
56 Stonewall and Centre for Family Research at the University of Cambridge (2017) School Report. Available at: https://www.stonewall.org.uk/syst em/files/the_school_report_2017.pdf
57 Toomey, R.B., Syvertsen, A.K. and Shramko, M. (2018) Transgender adolescent suicide behavior. Pediatrics, 124 (4), e20174218.

58 Biggs, M. (2022) Suicide by clinic-referred transgender adolescents in the United Kingdom. *Archives of Sexual Behavior*, 51 (2), 685–90.

59 National Center for Transgender Equality (2010) Preventing transgender suicide. Available at: https://web.archive.org/web/20150213054306/http:/transequality.org/PDFs/NCTE_Suicide_Prevention.pdf

60 For example, the claim that it is better to have a trans child than a dead one. Example: WYNC Studios (2016) I'd Rather Have a Living Son Than a Dead Daughter. Available at: https://www.wnycstudios.org/podcasts/onlyhuman/episodes/id-rather-have-living-son-dead-daughter

61 Samaritans. Samaritans' media guidelines. Available at: https://www.samaritans.org/about-samaritans/media-guidelines/

62 Twitter. @samaritans (2016) '1/3 or transgender adults and 1/2 young trans people attempt suidcide. This #WSPD gives a little love to those most at risk. 5.30 pm, 9 September. Available at: twitter.com/samaritans/status/774283915636805635?lang=en-GB

63 Varrella, S. (2022) Share of people identifying as transgender, gender fluid, non-binary, or other ways worldwide as of 2021, by country. Statista. Available at https://www.statista.com/statistics/1269778/gender-identity-worldwide-country/

64 Flores, A.R., Herman, J.L., Gates, G.J., et al. (2016) *How Many Adults Identify as Transgender in the United States?* Los Angeles, CA: The Williams Institute.

65 TGEU (2021) TVT TMM update • Trans Day of Remembrance 2021. Available at: https://transrespect.org/en/tmm-update-tdor-2021/

66 UNDOC (2018) Global study on homicide: Gender-related killing of women and girls. Available at https://www.unodc.org/documents/data-and-analysis/GSH2018/GSH18_Gender-related_killing_of_women_and_girls.pdf

67

	Estimated number of trans people at 1% to 3% of global population				Homicides per year	Deaths/ head/ population			
1%	1%	1.5%	2%	3%		1%	1.5%	2%	3%
						1 trans homicide per xxx people	1 trans homicide per xxx people	1 trans homicide xxx people	1 trans per homicide per xxx
7,980,178,081	79,801,781	119,072,671	159,603,562	239,405,342	375	212,805	319,207	425,609	638,414
3,953,737,839					87,000	45,445	45,445	45,445	45,445
						4.68	7.02	9.37	14.05
If 74% of the female population is over 16									
2,925,766,001					87,000	33,629	33,629	33,629	33,629
						6.33	9.49	12.66	18.98

68 Statista (2021) Proportion of selected age groups of world population in 2021, by region. Available at: https://www.statista.com/statistics/265759/world-population-by-age-and-region/
69 'Transrespect versus Transphobia Worldwide' (TvT) Trans Murder Monitoring 2020. Available at:https://transrespect.org/en/map/trans-murder-monitoring/?submap=tmm_2020
70 Gocompare (2021) The UK's riskiest jobs: found highest risk of death in jobs was for construction workers. Available at: https://www.gocompare.com/life-insurance/uk-riskiest-jobs-report/
71 As of 31 July 2022, Counting Dead Women.
72 Fair Play for Women (2021) UK police record male rapists as female under self-ID policy. Available at: https://fairplayforwomen.com/police_record_males_as_female/
73 Fair Play for Women (2021) Fair Play for Women wins High Court challenge and judge orders sex must not be self-identified in the Census. Available at: https://fairplayforwomen.com/fair-play-for-women-wins-high-court-challenge-against-ons-census/
74 Dodds, I. (2022) Home Office asks police to record trans people using their birth sex in crime statistics. The Independent, 12 April. Available at: https://www.independent.co.uk/news/uk/home-news/home-office-trans-crime-statistics-grc-birth-sex-b2056345.html
75 Ibid.

Chapter 8: Despatches from 'Terf Island'
1 Weldon, S.L. and Htun, M. (2013) Feminist mobilisation and progressive policy change: why governments take action to combat violence against women. Gender & Development, 21 (2), 231–47.
2 FINA (2022) Policy on eligibility for the men's and women's competition categories. Available at: https://resources.fina.org/fina/document/2022/06/19/525de003-51f4-47d3-8d5a-716dac5f77c7/FINA-INCLUSION-POLICY-AND-APPENDICES-FINAL-.pdf
3 FINA (2022) Press release: FINA announces new policy on gender inclusion. 19 June. Available at: https://www.fina.org/news/2649715/press-release-fina-announces-new-policy-on-gender-inclusion
4 Bell, K. (2021) My story. Persuasion, 7 April. Available at: https://www.persuasion.community/p/keira-bell-my-story?s=r
5 BBC (2022) Prime Minister Boris Johnson says transgender women should not compete in women's sport. BBC, 6 April. Available at: https://www.bbc.co.uk/sport/61012030
6 Egerton, J. (2021) Women and the religious right. The Radical Notion, Autumn.

7 Chrisafis, A., Connolly, K. and Giuffrida, A. (2019) From Le Pen to Alice Weidel: how the European far-right set its sights on women. *The Guardian*, 29 January. Available at: https://www.theguardian.com/life andstyle/2019/jan/29/from-le-pen-to-alice-weidel-how-the-european-far-right-set-its-sights-on-women

8 L'opinion (2016) Marine Le Pen: Un référendum pour sortir de la crise migratoire. 13 January. Available at: https://www.lopinion.fr/politique /marine-le-pen-un-referendum-pour-sortir-de-la-crise-migratoire

9 Queen Mary University of London. Mile End Institute (2015) UKIP uses women's rights as a trojan horse to attack minorities. Available at: https://www.qmul.ac.uk/mei/news-and-opinion/2015/items/ukip-uses -womens-rights-as-a-trojan-horse-to-attack-minorities.html

10 Doyle, J.E.S. (2022) How the far-right is turning feminists into fascists. Xtra, 1 April. Available at: https://xtramagazine.com/power/far-right -feminist-fascist-220810

11 Ibid.

12 Yasmin Alibhai-Brown demolishes gender-apartheidist Saleem Chagtai. Nicky Campbell, 25 November 2013, Radio 5 Live. Available at: https:// www.youtube.com/watch?v=0UStOCF4PFk

13 Alibhai-Brown, Y. (2013) It's shameful that our universities have accepted gender segregation under pressure from the most oppressive religious fanatics. *Independent*, 8 December. Available at: https://www.indepen dent.co.uk/voices/comment/it-s-shameful-that-our-universities-have-accepted-gender-segregation-under-pressure-from-the-most-oppres sive-religious-fanatics-8991593.html

14 Labour Campaign for Trans Rights. Available at: https://docs.google .com/forms/d/e/1FAIpQLSd_wPyenUicSJgKv1YTknZ47gDGU4b_389z YbqH10TGSTRrpg/viewform

15 Dawn Butler interview on *ITV Good Morning*, 16 February 2020.

16 Sex Matters (2021) We are worthy of respect in a democratic society. Available at: https://sex-matters.org/posts/updates/gender-critical-belie fs-are-worthy-of-respect-in-a-democratic-society/

17 Twitter @BluskyeAllison 27 July 2022. Available at: twitter.com/ BluskyeAllison/status/1552250836448837633

18 Rise up. Find out more at: https://brightonriseup.wordpress.com/

19 Lawrie, E. (2021) Ruling limiting under-16s puberty blockers overturned. BBC, 17 September. Available at: https://www.bbc.co.uk/news/uk-5859 8186

20 BBC (2021) NHS child gender identity clinic whistleblower wins tribu-nal. BBC, 5 September. Available at: https://www.bbc.co.uk/news/uk-58 453250

21 https://twitter.com/8RosarioSanchez/status/1517117006537019392
22 Cloisters (2021) Reindorf Review on 'no platforming'. Available at: https://www.cloisters.com/reindorf-review-on-no-platforming/
23 Julie Bindel settles libel claim with PinkNews (2021). Available at: https://www.5rb.com/news/julie-bindel-settles-libel-claim-with-pinknews/
24 Fair Play For Women (2021) Fair Play For Women wins High Court challenge and judge orders sex must not be self-identified in the Census. Available at: https://fairplayforwomen.com/fair-play-for-women-wins-high-court-challenge-against-ons-census/
25 Judiciary of Scotland (2022) *For Women Scotland v. the LA & the Scottish Ministers*. Available at: https://www.judiciary.scot/home/sentences-judgments/judgments/2022/02/18/for-women-scotland-v-the-la-the-scottish-ministers
26 Adapted to remove the male default from Karl Marx's 'From each according to his ability, to each according to his needs.' Marx, K. (2008 [1875]) *Critique of the Gotha Program*. Rockville, MD: Wildside Press.